ADOLFO RAMÍREZ CORONA

When I Grow up I Want to Be a UX Designer, Dad

Stories and reflections on a newly born profession

First edition

This book was professionally typeset on Reedsy.
Find out more at reedsy.com

To Ale, Fénix, and Luciana,
for the best and most important human experience
—a family

Contents

Foreword

I want to thank Fabricio Teixeira from **UX Collective** and Yenson Lau from **Toward Data Science** as the editors of the first published version of these works—as indicated in each piece.

The rest were published on **Medium** and **Concepts Against Reality**.

All the articles were updated in the external URLs, obsolete references, and little corrections.

Preface

What does a smartphone smell like?

What is the difference between users, customers, and audiences?

How complex is a profession like UX that is not easy to explain to a 5-year-old, like explaining what a firefighter or an architect does?

What is the difference between designing app experiences and writing for TV or movies?

How can a product or brand have the thing that makes a song so memorable?

How much do you have to surprise your users versus how much do you need to make them comfortable and secure?

These questions are part of the journey documented in this book, a journey through the world of UX, UI, apps, and digital design. It is narrated by someone whose first choice after high school was Philosophy. Later, after discovering a passion for "art" through photography, he decided to become an artist. However, it was the fields of math and technology that paid the bills, leading him to delve into statistics, TV ratings, media, engineering, app development, and software development. Alongside these technical pursuits, he also pursued a humanistic side of life and work, becoming a psychotherapist.

But, most importantly, he was someone who encountered the world of UX, embarking on a journey of learning and self-discovery. This journey coincided with life-altering experiences, such as starting new relationships, becoming a stepparent, and becoming a parent.

Expect to encounter technical aspects of UX, infused with colloquial and conversational philosophy, as well as personal and family anecdotes. For this writer, it is impossible to discuss the dark mode on UI without recalling the experiences of using a cell phone while putting his daughter to sleep. Or to consider the different smells of a smartphone used in a hospital versus a restaurant. Or to write interfaces while reflecting on French semiotics. Or to choose between a figurative or minimalist design while contemplating people's preferences for nonfiction or fiction stories.

* * *

I, the author, began writing and publishing in English on Medium in March 2018. Initially, my focus was on philosophical and psychotherapeutic topics. However, as had often been the case in my life, I couldn't resist commenting on technology-related matters. Unsurprisingly, people found my thoughts on technology more enticing than mindfulness or emotions (at least until personal problems arose, leading them to seek my help).

The articles on UX received the most positive responses. Fabricio Teixeira, the editor of *UX Collective*, read one of their articles—The Future of the Smartphone Is Not the Smartphone—and invited me to publish with the publication. During this collaboration, I penned and published more articles on UX than any other subject.

Looking back at all the articles published during these years,

I realized that some had become outdated quickly—those pertaining to Twitter, for example. Yet others withstood the test of time and became personal references for my ideas, stories, and reflections on the subject.

In this book, you will find a curated and updated selection of those articles, organized by topic: UX origins and foundations, UX designing and thinking, UX writing and other skills, and objects and products.

Lastly, I wrote and published the article that gives the book its title, When I Grow Up I Want to Be a UX Designer, Dad, when my youngest daughter was four years old. Today, she is seven and aspires to be a teacher like her mom. I'm still unsure how to convince her how great, interesting, enriching, and cool working in the field of UX can be.

It is my hope that this book will successfully convey the idea to you.

August 2023

I

On UX origins and foundations

1

When I grow up I want to be a UX designer, dad

On emerging professions and their place in society

It's hard to imagine a child saying that s/he wants to be a UX designer when s/he grows up. Why?

Let's try to explain to a five-year-old what a UX designer does.

You can talk just about some aspects of the profession, like, "a UX designer researches like a scientific", or, "a UX designer makes things easy to use".

Or you can talk about the product of the process, like, "A UX designer designs apps". But UX design is more than research or designing apps, right?

Is this a problem of overgeneralization or overspecialization[1] of the profession? Does a UX designer make too specific things or make too many?

> *...when it comes to design, there's no such thing as ultimate guides, magic formulas, or UX unicorns. There's a lot of discipline and hard work, that's what there is. —Fabricio Teixeira[2]*

You can use a lot of analogies to explain what a UX designer does but you can't resume it with a simple description.

"It's like building things with Lego...", doesn't differentiate a UX designer from the architect.

Or, "it's like inventing games for the computer", is something you can say for a software engineer or a game designer.

The easy solution can be to forget about the "UX" factor and explain what a designer is. But the design is too general!

We can explain what a UI designer does, and I can perfectly imagine a kid playing to be one.

Or, we can explain what a UX writer does, and I can also imagine someone playing doing that.

But UX design is a career you think about later in your life. Maybe after beginning another career.

UX design isn't a job like that of a firefighter, mechanic,

---

[1] Teixeira, Fabricio. "You Don't Need to Know Everything about UX." Medium, April 25, 2018. https://uxdesign.cc/you-dont-need-to-know-everything-about-ux-9b7abd686ef0.

[2] "Our Industry Needs More Designers. Most Importantly: A Different Type of Designer. | by Fabricio Teixeira | Bootcamp." Accessed March 15, 2023. https://bootcamp.uxdesign.cc/our-industry-needs-more-designers-most-importantly-a-different-type-of-designer-dc98cfae4411.

lawyer, doctor, engineer, software programmer, gardener, scientist, architect, lawyer, manager, marketer, baker, mathematician, barber, teacher... or even philosopher.

Or, what did a UX designer play when s/he was a child? I can't imagine a kid saying, "I'll be the UX designer", after another one choosing "nurse" or "accountant".

A kid can play a lot of jobs and professions. In fact, role-playing is a great form of learning by doing. What does a UX designer do that can't be role-played?

> *If you can't explain it simply, you don't understand it*
> *well enough. —Albert Einstein*

Two emerging professions from the immediate past

In the 1980s, there was a career fair at my high school. There were stands and talks. One of the most popular careers was Communication. In those years, the big companies were the media companies. Politicians feared the press, radio, and TV as today they fear Facebook, Google, or Twitter.

One of the talks was hosted by Communication students. It was full. Everybody wanted to know about the career of the future.

You could tell that the expositor was very proud of his profession because he did a very comprehensive description of it.

But as the talk went on, the description of what a Communication specialist does started to be confusing. Writing, designing, filming, photographing, presenting, showing... for radio, TV, movies, books, magazines, newspapers, talks, illustration, manuals, training, signaling, music, architecture, art, government...

Most of the assistants were thinking the same, I guess. A communicator knows about writing but there are writers that actually write. Or a communicator knows about designing but there are designers that actually design. And so on.

At some moment, one of my high schoolmates raised his hand, expressed his confusion, and asked the expositor: "Could you define to us what communication is?".

The expositor, still proud, answered, "Communication is everything", with the special emphasis you put in the word "everything" when saying "We are everything" or "God is everything".

That day was my last interest in the career of Communication. It seemed too pretentious. We started to call the communicologists, "allologists", specialists in all. And no kid said in those years, "When I grow up I want to be a communicologist", for sure.

I liked some of the things that were part of the Communication field— I already loved to write—but why would I study design or TV if I wanted to be a writer? (Oh, if I had known...)

The truth is that Communication stopped being a trend. It was, at that moment, an emerging profession, a consequence of the necessities of the industry. Media companies were growing and they needed personnel. Not specialized personnel but general personnel. A communicologist that could specialize once s/he was on the job.

Today young people prefer to study filming, photography, creative writing, design (in any of its multiple specialties, including UX), publishing...

The opposite happened with System Engineers. The position in a company for a Systems Engineer (or similar, like Engineering Informatics) was restricted to what the few computers of a company could accomplish, which, in those years, was only some accounting.

During the 1990s and 2000s, the position of Systems Engineer went from accounting support to became what today we call the CTO or CIO, just under — and sometimes next to — the CEO.

And I remember children saying, "When I grow up I want to be a computer engineer".

It's fair to say that both Communication and Systems Engineering were careers covering a wide variety of areas of knowledge. When digitization began in industries, the requirement of technology "generalists" increased. You might be a good software programmer but once you were hired, the company needed you to supervise the installation of the new Ethernet network. And you did it. That's why the position grew to be one of the most important in any business.

Now, I imagine a Systems Engineer saying to that Communicologist in the career fair, "Technology and information are everything."

An emerging profession at the present

UX design is an emerging profession, there is no doubt about it. But, it is an emerging profession that it's going to dissolve into different specialties like Communication did or is it going to grow as Systems Engineering did?

If we look at the stories published today in UX Collective,[3]

---

[3] Medium. "UX Collective Editors." Accessed March 15, 2023. https://uxdesigncc.medium.com.

for instance, we can see a very wide list of topics, from writing, interfaces, marketing, planning, research, animation, AI, soft skills, psychology, content, branding, strategy, Figma...

Is UX design growing and expanding its domains — we can see UX positions in industries that we didn't think about ten years ago — or dividing into its branches — a UX designer isn't enough for some companies and they hire UX writers, UI designers, UX researchers, etc.?

Or maybe I'm missing something here and children are understanding better what a UX designer is as they interact more and more with apps, games, distant learning, and digital worlds.

Of course, this digression is not about children. This digression came to my mind thinking about how easy it is for my wife to explain what she does — teaching — to our four-year-old when I can't explain to our fourteen-year-old what I do.

Well, I can explain her in some way, but the point is that it made me think about the place our professions have in our society and industry and how they have changed over time.

Or maybe I just don't understand UX design well enough because I can't explain it simply as Einstein said.

I'll keep learning.

(Published on Jul 22, 2020, in UX Collective)

2

UX is about the X, not the U

The design challenge is in the human factor of the equation

There is no "user experience design", only "experience design". The only ones enabled to experience are humans. User experience design was born at the engineering campus, from the perspective of machines, computers, and apparatus. The intruder in the informatics and mechanical field was an entity capable of experiencing things. They called it "user".

It's time to make a correction: we design experiences, and experiences can only live by humans — as far as we know — so to include the word "user" is an unnecessary pleonasm.

I invented the term because I thought human interface and usability were extremely good. I wanted to cover all aspects of the person's experience with the system including industrial design graphics, the interface, the physical interaction and the manual. Since then the term has spread widely, so much so that it is starting to gain its meaning. —Donald Norman[4]

The word "user" in UX simply resumes three other words: human-computer interaction.

Some have found the word "user" unnecessary before but for different reasons. And yes, we have to eliminate the word user because, as Adam Lefton has written, it "reduces humans to a single behavior, effectively supporting a view of people as more like robots whose sole function is to use a product or feature".[5]

But in addition to that, consider that the concept of "user" was born within the engineering field where an interface or an interaction can be between different elements in a system—elements that can be devices, servers, clients, or users.

The innovation wasn't in the U-word, as Lefton calls it, but in bringing a word from the Psychology field to the engineering one: experience. Within the concept of "experience", the "user" is implied.

Once user experience design was a new field itself, I heard that the term Human-Centered Design should substitute User Experience Design, because users are humans. But the word "human", even though is a beautiful and humanistic word, is unnecessary because "human" is also implicit in the design of

---

[4] "User Experience Design." In *Wikipedia*, February 21, 2023. https://en.wiki pedia.org/w/index.php?title=User_experience_design&oldid=114063339 4.

[5] Lefton, Adam. "As a Designer, I Refuse to Call People 'Users.'" *Medium* (blog), January 24, 2019. https://medium.com/s/user-friendly/why-im-done-saying-user-user-experience-and-ux-in-2019-4fdfc6b7de23.

experiences.

And there is a fundamental problem if we take away the concept of experience from the definition. As I said, the main insight and value of Don Norman's legacy is the inclusion of "experience" in design. We might find a better word for the concept of "experience", or even expand the concept and use another term, but the original concept can't be eliminated.

Don Norman deprecated the use of the word "users" in an article from 2008:

> Words matter. Psychologists depersonalize the people they study by calling them "subjects." We depersonalize the people we study by calling them "users." Both terms are derogatory. They take us away from our primary mission: to help people. —Don Norman[6]

In that case, the word that can be eliminated from "user experience design" is "user". But if we call it just "experience design" it can be confused with an old and obsolete distinction between those terms.

User experience design vs Experience design

In the recent past, there have been attempts to separate user experience design (UXD) from experience design (XD). The main reason is a division of functions and goals that are unsustainable today. Let's see them.

---

6   jnd.org. "Words Matter. Talk About People: Not Customers, Not Consumers, Not Users," November 17, 2008. https://jnd.org/words_matter_talk_abo ut_people_not_customers_not_consumers_not_users/.

The main distinction you may find googling the terms is that UXD is for designing digital products and XD is for any kind of product and the whole environment in which they are consumed.

In that sense, UXD is just part of XD.

The problem with this distinction today is that the line between digital products and products, services, processes, or events is thin or inexistent.

What is a digital product? Uber? Uber app or the food delivery service? Is the app UXD and the service XD?

Or what about the apps that some departmental stores have? They are not designed only to shop online but to extend the experience of buying in the physical store to the app.

And the list can be unlimited. Airlines apps try to be a companion throughout your trip. Airbnb not only gets you a place to sleep but experiences living in the surroundings. Or Apple Pay was born as a digital service under the name of iTunes or App Store but now breaks the digital third wall to be used at any point of sale.

I found another distinction between UXD and XD that says that while the user wants to accomplish something, the experiencer wants to feel something.[7]

But let's think about meditation apps. UXD or XD? Does the user of a meditation app want to accomplish something without feeling? Or does s/he want to feel something without accomplishing anything?

The boundaries here are also obsolete.

---

[7] Bell, Ashleigh. "UX vs XD ... Users vs Humans." *QDivision* (blog), May 24, 2017. https://medium.com/qdivision/ux-vs-xd-users-vs-humans-773d00035935.

Another distinction has been made saying that in UXD only some senses are involved — vision, tact, and hearing, I guess — and in XD all the senses are involved. But, What does a smartphone smell like? While it is true that a user interface doesn't smell per se, it can enable the involvement of all the senses in the experience.

A good example is again in the meditation apps. There are meditations of the five senses where you are guided through the mindful perception of your senses.

Today the user experience design transcends the bidimen-sionality of the user interface.

The day UX design and XD became one

At some point, the distinction between UXD and XD became obsolete and a merge came. To be more precise, the merge was on April 13 of 2019 at 01:17 hours.[8]

Screenshot from Wikipedia

---

8 "User Experience Design (2019)." In *Wikipedia*, April 13, 2019. https://en. wikipedia.org/w/index.php?title=User_experience_design&oldid=89222 6746.

GenQuest, the Wikipedia editor that did the merge, found an evident overlap in both entries, UX and XD. The overlap might be not evident at the beginning—the first appearance of UX as an article in Wikipedia was in 2006.[9]

But with the merge what disappeared was the concept of "experience design" without the "user".

Like most encyclopedias and dictionaries, Wikipedia tries to reflect the current use of terms and concepts and avoids proposing new ones.

The use of UXD over XD has prevailed, and GenQuest was right in the merge, although a big brand and community like Adobe have adopted the XD instead. UXD or UX design is the term most of us in the field are using. But is it the correct one?

The X in job listings

In terms of job listings is another story.[10] There are user experience designers, product experience designers, customer experience designers, brand experience designers, employee experience designers, user experience ecosystem designers, or even user experience generalist designers, (wait, what?).

UXD, XD, CX, BX, PX, UXG, EX, UXE...

---

[9] "User Experience Design (2006)." In *Wikipedia*, November 15, 2006. https://en.wikipedia.org/w/index.php?title=User_experience_design&oldid=87907180.

[10] "UX vs. CX vs. XD? Analyzing 17 Years of User Experience Job Titles | LinkedIn." Accessed March 15, 2023. https://www.linkedin.com/pulse/ux-vs-cx-xd-analyzing-17-years-user-experience-job-titles-colin-eagan/.

Randall Smith from the agency modern8[11] calls it "the x factor".[12] The importance of experience has permeated all the disciplines around design. And that is good.

The truth is that once the boundaries between all the X disciplines or areas, the same happens in the day-to-day job.

You might start designing the experience for an app that was sold as a product in an app store. But then, the business model changed and now the app is available as a subscription. So, the app is just a product for a service, the user becomes a customer, and the experience goes beyond the screen.

Or you start designing the customer experience for a physical shop, but then an app is produced to complement or expand the experience. Then, the sales are higher on the app than in the store, so you must redesign the experience all the way around.

Or you start designing a meditation or an ambient music app for calming or focusing. Then the demand for more and diverse content is required—music, DJs, teachers, coaches. You become designing the experience for content that suits those needs, and you become a sort kind of content experience designer.

The U is here to stay, but...

I know, it's impossible to change the fact that the use of the term "user experience" is here to stay. It's the term that has survived, it's in the books and tutorials, job listings, internet

---

[11] modern8. "Brand by Design." Accessed March 15, 2023. https://modern8.com/.

[12] Smith, Randall. "The x Factor." *Modern8* (blog), May 29, 2018. https://modern8.com/the-x-factor/.

domains, Wikipedia, and in our daily life.

But at least we must be conscious that we design experiences. No matter at which point of the experience we start to design, in the end, the people need us to think about the whole experience or usability, consumption, costuming, environment, with products, services, events, processes, apps, printing, interfaces, text, voice, images...

And everybody in this field needs to learn about every aspect of the experience. I don't know if the right word is "generalist", but while you need to specialize in one aspect of the experience, you need to be interested and open-minded about the parts that aren't your area of expertise.

This is important: specialization becomes by contrast. The only way you can recognize what makes a feature or a person special or unique is to be aware of the whole other features or people. To find a niche in the market you must know the market. To identify a particular tree you must know the forest.

Do interface designers need to learn to program? Do programmers need to learn to interface design? If learning helps you to understand better the experience, yes.

But more design and more programming can help you with the U factor — the interface element —, not necessarily with the X factor — the human factor. Psychology, communication, marketing, sales, neuroscience, and market research, are nearer to help you understand the X factor. Humans are the complex part of the formula to understand.

And humans are in the X, not in the U.

> *People are rich, complex beings. They use our devices with specific goals, motives, and agendas. Often they work with — or against — others. A label such as cus-*

tomer, consumer or user ignores this rich structure of abilities, motives, and social structures. —Don Norman[13]

(Published on Jun 15, 2020, in UX Collective)

---

[13] jnd.org. "Words Matter. Talk About People: Not Customers, Not Consumers, Not Users," November 17, 2008. https://jnd.org/words_matter_talk_abo ut_people_not_customers_not_consumers_not_users/.

3

What was before the user?

On consumers, audiences and users, and why we need to know about it

Where does the concept of user come from? Before the concept of the user was the concept of the audience. And before that, it was the concept of the consumer.

Concepts help us to understand reality. When reality changes, we need new concepts. When reality—or part of it—becomes too complex, we need complex concepts.

Concepts are powerful tools to understand and transform reality.

> *A concept is a brick. It can be used to build a courthouse of reason. Or it can be thrown through the window.—*

Gilles Deleuze and Felix Guattari, A Thousand Plateaus[14]

We are talking about users now. But the concept of the user is relatively new. We didn't communicate, market, or design to users thirty years ago.

Carl Sagan used to say that you have to know the past to understand the present. Let's do that.

The consumer era

In the old era, the economy was based on the consumer, and so was marketing and design.

We are talking about from the beginning of the industrialized world to the post-second-war years.

The consumer was the individual that bought products or services. The economy was built around this premise. Any business goal was to bring consumers to buy products or services.

At that time, the products and services were physical — made of unwieldy atoms, Negroponte *dixit*[15] — so the companies hired professionals to move the consumers to their stores.

The industrialized world was able to use the advantages of mass production, so it needed to use mass communication for mass sales.

Big money was in the hands of the mass-production industry.

Communicators, marketers, and designers were to create

---

[14] "*A Thousand Plateaus.*" In *Wikipedia*, March 14, 2023. https://en.wikipedia.org/w/index.php?title=A_Thousand_Plateaus&oldid=1144584864.

[15] "*Being Digital.*" In *Wikipedia*, February 14, 2023. https://en.wikipedia.org/w/index.php?title=Being_Digital&oldid=1139348267.

awareness of the products and services, build interest in them, generate desire for them, and finally, make the consumers take action to buy them.

Yes, that's the old A.I.D.A[16] marketing model for awareness, interest, desire, and action.

Note that the way from creating awareness to action was a straight line. Note also that the goal was to make the consumers take *one* action.

That was the Mad Men era. Did you want to sell a new car model? You had to produce a mass campaign for newspapers, magazines, street boards, radio, and television... just to communicate a message. The marketing mix. This was also the publishing era. The communication was mainly in one direction, from the sender to the receiver.

In those times it was very difficult to know the actual effectiveness of advertising, marketing, and design.

As is today with the economy that uses that model, it's very difficult to know if a consumer that buys a product or service is doing it because he heard, saw, or read a specific ad.

How many ads do you place? How frequently? How long? Do we place different versions of the ad?

There were standard answers for those questions which were born in market research, but to be the truth, it was a very inaccurate science.

---

[16] "AIDA (Marketing)." In *Wikipedia*, November 6, 2022. https://en.wikipedia.org/w/index.php?title=AIDA_(marketing)&oldid=1120318560.

The audience era

In the beginning, radio, television, and cinema were children of the minstrels and troubadours. They brought some entertainment to the town square where the people were gathering.

If you wanted to communicate some message to the town, you went to the town square, do some entertainment, and tell your message.

But entertainment became an industry and a big business. Every newspaper, magazine, film study, radio or television channel, started to build their audience.

We left the mass production era to arrive at the mass communication era.

The concept of the audience was a little bit confusing in the beginning because the audience was treated like clients or consumers but they didn't pay anything (or almost anything) for the product or service they used.

For example, a television channel is used to produce content to serve the requirements of the audience. They put on the screen what the audience liked. So, in some sense, the audience was a consumer because the channel delivered them a product or service. But at the same time, the audience wasn't a consumer because they didn't pay.

But once you had an audience and their attention you had something to sell to businesses looking for consumers.

The economy of the consumer is changed by the economy of the audience. The consumer didn't disappear, of course, but the actual client of the mass media was the mass-production companies. And the audience was the product of the mass media.

This is very important to understand the current era: the

mass media industry gave content for free (and competed in that) to get more audience and better.

The communication, marketing, and design were according to that. The A.I.D.A model prevailed but we left the Mad Men era to the Hollywood era. Lifestyle, great content, emotional bond.

More than getting attention to get action, the design and marketing were to build trust and loyalty to a product or service. Getting an audience was very expensive, so once you got it you wanted to keep it.

For broadcasters, this was meant to create content that engaged the audience. For marketers and designers, this was meant to build a brand.

This was the broadcasting era. Publishing was like sending a letter to someone. Broadcasting was like throwing paper propaganda from an airplane: a lot of it was going to the trash, and only some of it got your audience.

Because you used to have too many channels and media outlets you needed market segments, targets, ergo different content for different audiences.

You needed to know your audience. Market research didn't disappear, of course, but this was the era of audience research.

Yet, the beginning of the internet was part of this era. The first web pages, sites, and portals, were looking for an audience. The browser's war (do you remember Netscape?) was an audience war.

Google understood it perfectly and built its business model—its first business model—according to that: the audience was the product.

The user era

We think basically you watch television to turn your brain off, and you work on your computer when you want to turn your brain on. —Steve Jobs[17]

But very soon, simple web pages gradually became more interactive. From the simple interaction that hypertext required to browse other pages, to more and more complex functions and applications between not just pages but sites, other users, databases, scripts, programs...

So the audience becomes the user. And now the confusion is often between products and services. These words are sometimes interchangeable. That is because we left the physical products and services to the digital ones.

Moreover, sometimes the product is the message. For example, for a TV program like *Stranger Things,* you develop an app that is a game just to promote your brand or create fans. Or to keep them engaged until the next season.

It's not enough to get attention, interest, desire, and *one* action from the people. It's not enough to build fidelity and loyalty to a brand. It's not enough to offer a lifestyle, great content, or emotional bond.

Your user (former consumer and audience) is going to interact with your product, your service, or your message, or all three, one behind the other. Or at the same time, for that matter. Marketing and design have to work accordingly.

In the end, that is why in this era you design experiences.

---

[17] "Steve Jobs - Wikiquote." Accessed March 15, 2023. https://en.wikiquote.org/wiki/Steve_Jobs.

The user buys like a consumer, watches as an audience, and interacts like a user.

Following the previous example, your user knows about the new TV series Stranger Things from an ad on Netflix. He reads about the casting or the directors in a web article. Watches the first episode on his smartphone, and later at home with his family. Visits the official website or Facebook Page. Shares images, and trailers on social networks. Plays the soundtrack on Spotify. Downloads the game just out of curiosity. Talks to his friends about it at a party. Reads more articles, now about the second season coming. Buys comics online. Discovers that there is a thematic apparel line. Etcetera.

We still have market and audience research. But today is the era of the web and data analytics. We know exactly which click or button made the sale. We don't have to figure out a marketing funnel because we know the actual marketing funnel.

This is the *deploy* era. You deploy a website, an app, a platform, a product a service. Even if you start an ad campaign, you really are deploying it. You do minimal design, preview, and publishing when you set your ads on Google. And the ads are going to be seen by the users depending on the rules you set.

Consequences

- The consumers, audiences, or users are, before all, humans. We publish, communicate, broadcast, market, design, and deploy, to humans.
- We are living the three eras at the same time, of course. None of them have disappeared. They are overlapping. We

have to understand them and use that understanding to communicate, market, or design.

· The most recent era adds elements, functions, and knowledge, to the previous one. You have to know how to start a traditional ad campaign as well as how to generate content and deploy a website. You have to know the A.I.D.A model and too many others.[18]

· The species in danger of extinction are the Mad Men and the Hollywood Men. No more seasons for campaigns or content. Deploying is a continuous and iterative process. Communicators, marketers, and designers are no longer specialists, but expert generalists.[19]

(Published on Nov 13, 2019, in UX Collective)

---

[18] Chaffey, Dave. "Marketing Models That Have Stood the Test of Time [Free Guide]." Smart Insights, November 24, 2022. https://www.smartinsights.com/digital-marketing-strategy/online-business-revenue-models/marketing-models/.

[19] Roberta. "Expert Generalist." Medium, May 9, 2020. https://uxdesign.cc/expert-generalist-f2a15eab400a.

4

3 variables you must know to understand your users better

Users, customers or audience: how many, how much, how often?

They have different names depending on the product or service, whether we talk about users, customers, or audience, a medium or a web platform, or the method to measure. But no matter if you own a restaurant, an app, or a TV broadcasting channel, you have to know them.

Don't worry, you don't need to be a mathematician to understand them.

The restaurant's model

Everybody has gone to that popular restaurant that it's always full of diners and difficult to get a table. You guess it's a success and you even secretly wanted to have a business like that.

But the number of customers is an incomplete measure.

What happens if every customer just asks for a cup of coffee? You may create the perfect experience for the clients, a great environment, and excellent service, but it may not be the goal of your service or product.

So, in a restaurant, the quantity of customers isn't enough to measure success. You need to know how much they spend on it.

Let's suppose the restaurant has a good quantity of customers and a good average spend per each. The concept is great and everybody wants to know the restaurant. In the first weeks, maybe in the first months, the restaurant is full of customers. But suddenly, one day you pass in front of it and discover it's empty. What happened?

Again, you created the best experience for the clients, a great environment, and excellent service, but for some reason, the customers don't return to the restaurant.

So, in a restaurant, the number of customers and how much they spend aren't enough variables to measure success. You need to know the frequency at which they come to the restaurant.

The same goes for a website, an app, a service, or a product.

1. Reach

You need to know how many users, customers, or audiences you have. For that, you need to define what a user, customer, or audience means.

In a restaurant, it could seem obvious. Every person pays a minimum amount of money. But be careful because you can have a person who pays but one or more that come with her or him and eat. You should measure diners.

A user can be the one who uses your app. But downloading isn't enough at these times, so you may define your user as a subscriber or based on some interaction within the app.

For TV and video, the audience is usually defined in terms of a minimum of seconds or minutes consumed, but in cinema in terms of tickets.[20]

In advertising and media,[21] you use the word *audience reach* meaning the total number of different people exposed, at least once, to a medium during a given period.[22]

In social media marketing, you use the term *social media reach* which refers to the number of users who have come across a particular content on a social platform.[23]

No matter if we talk about users, customers, or audiences, you have to know how many people you reach.

2. Average spend

Once you define your customers, you need to know how much they spend in your restaurant. In this case, you have to take into account every diner and not just the person who paid. That is called the *average spend per customer*, in general, and the *average spend per diner*, in the restaurant business.

In some cases, you want to increase the number of customers.

[20] "Audience Measurement." In *Wikipedia*, January 16, 2023. https://en.wikipedia.org/w/index.php?title=Audience_measurement&oldid=1134014663.

[21] Garnett, Christina. "What Is Audience Research? (+How to Conduct It)." Accessed March 23, 2023. https://learn.g2.com/audience-research.

[22] "Reach (Advertising)." In *Wikipedia*, March 3, 2023. https://en.wikipedia.org/w/index.php?title=Reach_(advertising)&oldid=1142572328.

[23] "Social Media Reach." In *Wikipedia*, November 3, 2022. https://en.wikipedia.org/w/index.php?title=Social_media_reach&oldid=1119710767.

But once you have enough customers (your tables are full), you want to increase the average spend per customer (or diner).

In the media, like TV, audio, or video, the currency of exchange is time. You may have heard about the attention economy. Well, the only way to measure how much attention your product or service gets is through the time the audience spends on it.

If you offer a podcast or a video 60 minutes long and the average time spent per person is 30 minutes, you say your content has a *fidelity* of 50%.

Once you have users or an audience, you want them to spend more time on your product or service.

The same goes for some online services or apps. In web analytics fidelity is called *average time on page.* But in most web and app cases, time is not the unity of measure because it doesn't make much sense.

Do you remember your user journey or your user flow? Or your marketing funnel? Well, you establish certain interactions through it and you measure how far your user goes. In games, for instance, you have levels or stages. On landing pages, you have stepped before the call to action.

In web analytics, besides the average time on the page, you have the number of sessions per user, average time per session... All of them are variations of the same concept.

However, no matter if you measure money, time, or actions, this is a variable that tries to measure a user's behavior related to your goals. Or, in other words, what the user does.

3. Frequency

In a restaurant, if you consider the bill or purchase of every customer as your first measure you are going to fail to identify customers and their behavior. In a week, for example, you can have a hundred bills or purchases. But that doesn't mean that you have a hundred customers. Some customers may come every morning for breakfast, others a couple of times a week.

Identifying customers helps you to measure important variables, like the percentage of *returning customers*. No matter how many times the customers have returned, how many of your customers are returning customers? 15%, 20%, 50%?[24]

But most importantly, you can calculate the *purchase frequency*, the average of times your customers have returned in a given period.

For a restaurant, you may use periods of weeks or months. For example, your customers come to your restaurant 2 times a month. Just remember we are talking about averages. You have heavy customers that come almost every weekday and customers that never come back.

How do you identify customers and not about billing or purchases in the case of physical shops? Well, have you seen those "custom loyalty cards"? One of the advantages of loyalty programs is the data you can get from them.

In media and advertising, you also have a frequency as the number of times a person is exposed to content. This is important in advertising because in order to deliver an

---

[24] "Repeat Purchase Rate, and How to Calculate It - Shopify Apps and Advice." Accessed March 23, 2023. https://www.littlestreamsoftware.com/articles/repeat-purchase-rate-calculate/.

ad message the audience needs to see it more than once. Depending on the content — from a simple brand message to a specific promotion with instructions — a campaign may need more or less frequency.

On websites and apps, you have return visitors or users. You may have heard the term "active users" in social networks or subscription services. Sometimes the number of users isn't enough, and you want to define your users as those who have used the service or logged-in in a given period.

Similar to the case with the restaurant example and its purchases versus customers, in the web and apps you may have a lot of views, downloads, or any defined interaction, but it's important to identify the actual users. Some of the views, downloads, or interactions can be done by the same user more than once.

Variables have variation

This is just an introduction to 3 basic variables to know your users. Take into consideration that once you have data for these variables you can measure variations or segments within them and not just averages.[25]

For instance, you can classify different kinds of customers or users according to how much money they spend, how frequently they come, or under any useful demographic like genre, age, scholarly, etc. A *target* is a specific demographic. Do you want to sell more to teenagers? Well, you define teenagers

---

[25] Moran, Melissa. "Why Your Variables Need to Vary." Statistics Solutions, August 14, 2017. https://www.statisticssolutions.com/why-your-variable s-need-to-vary/.

as your target and start measuring their behavior.

Or you can identify your heavy users and try to understand their characteristics versus your light users. The sky is the limit when you start playing with data.

Remember

Knowing your users, customers or audience is fundamental to offering a better service, product, content, or experience. These are the 3 basic variables that work for any kind of business.

Next time, try to use the restaurant example as a reference: number of diners, payment amount per each, and return frequency.

On some level, these variables are intuitive for any person owning a restaurant or a shop. But on other levels, they can give us a lot of information for decision-making if we understand them and exploit them.

(Published on Mar 21, 2020, in Towards Data Science)

5

The interface is the message and good design is invisible

Between McLuhan's Gutenberg Galaxy and Norman's Everyday Things

In 1993, a new printed magazine was presented at the Mac-World conference. Wired Magazine became the referent for the chronicle and understanding of emergent technologies and their effects on culture and society.

Wired had a techno-utopic spirit, a nerdy almost high-brow rhetoric, and a big influence from Marshall McLuhan's way to approach popular culture through the eyes of critical theory.

In fact, the media theorist was called by the magazine its "patron saint".

To understand the present reality, the best we can use is the theories of the immediate past.

Looking for answers to understand the upcoming digital age Wired was writing about, a man who died more than ten years

33

before (1980) was the one suited for the task.

Technology and communication were two of the main topics in McLuhan's works. So it was no accident that some of his concepts and rhetorics were used to describe and explain the arrival of computers, software, and the internet to society and culture.

With McLuhan, we were talking about computers and the internet as the new movable type printer. How a machine changes society.

The media theorists weren't trying to change reality, just trying to explain it.

From Cognitive Engineering to User Experience Design

Today, we try to understand new technologies in a more specific way. We talk about apps, interfaces, platforms, social networks, users, and experiences.

The electronics and mechanisms were left in a black box, and designers arrived at the scene, bringing with them a wider approach to the new field and culture.

Designers talk about objects in general—no matter if an object is an app, a website, a smartphone, a virtual assistant, etc.—and their interactions with people.

Designers, unlike media theorists, aren't passive observers. They don't ask how this is but how it could be.

Perception, cognition, experience, habits, behavior, and consciousness, are some of the interactions between object and user. Therefore, with designers, psychologists came too.

In 1993—yes, the same year Wired appeared—a Psychologist with a background in Engineering, joined Apple Computer as a User Experience Architect.

Don Norman was known for an article titled "The truth about Unix: The user interface is horrid", which he wrote in 1981, not just about how the Unix interface was, but how the interface should be. He still used the term Cognitive Engineering and not User Experience Design:

> *Cognitive Engineering is a new discipline, so new that it*
> *doesn't exist: but it ought to. Quite a bit is known about*
> *the human information processing system, enough that*
> *we can specify some basic principles for designers. —Don*
> *Norman, 1981*[26]

Most of the theory we use to explain the new technology today comes from Don Norman putting into practice part of his ideas working with Apple then and Hewlett-Packard and Nielsen Norman Group later.

His most famous book and the Bible of the UX field, *The Design of Everyday Things*, was published in 2013.

The interface is the message

"The medium is the message" is one of the most famous quotes in media theory and one of the less understood.

Marshall McLuhan states that we can't separate content and form, figure and ground, or, as quoted, medium and message.

We usually see the message, content, or figure, and we forget about the medium, ground, or form.

---

[26] Donald A., Norman. "The Truth about Unix: The User Interface Is Horrid." *Datamation*, 1981.

The figure doesn't just need the container or vehicle to be noticed but the container or vehicle gives form to the figure.

Let's think about content: a novel. A novel is "a relatively long work of narrative fiction, normally written in prose form, and which is typically published as a book" (Wikipedia[27]).

First, the "relativity" of the longness comes from technical aspects of the book as an object, such as paper size, bound, printing, and distribution, more than aesthetical aspects.

Before a printing book was a commercial option, there was serialized fiction published in journals every week or month.

Like the modern TV series, every new episode had to be readable without knowing all the previous chapters. Most of all, every installment had to leave an attractive cliffhanger to motivate future purchases.

They were a very efficient commercial option for a particular audience with no habits for books.

The origin and history of what we call a novel today depend on the publishing technology and the distribution systems that enable it.

A modern novel is written to be published in book form. The narrative, the rhythm, and the style are influenced by this.

In other words, we can't understand a novel just as content. The medium, ground, or form are part of what a novel is.

The medium is the message.

When we talk about design, the same happens. Design is not just a vehicle for a message. It's a message itself.

---

[27] "Novel." In *Wikipedia*, May 17, 2023. https://en.wikipedia.org/w/index.ph p?title=Novel&oldid=1155301005.

Good design is invisible

"When you don't notice the music in a movie, the music is good", told us a high school teacher like he was reveling in a life secret. A good teacher because, no matter if true, I always remembered that statement.

Form, figure, container... pick the name, can't be completely invisible. If you can't see the form you can't see the content.

But there are grades of information.

When a coworker tells you about a new company's project, the story is the content. Your coworker, with his inflections, accent, and style, it's the form, a form with extra information.

But let's suppose that your coworker doesn't speak a language you understand. You use a third person as a translator. So, the story is basically the same, but now you have to add the extra information added by the translation and the translator.

In both cases, you can't know the company's new project unless your coworker tells it. The extra information is inevitable and necessary.

The interface design carries extra information because it's a vehicle. How much extra information? It depends on the sender, receiver, message, context, channel...

Or, in other words, it depends on the usability goals, the user characteristics, the environment, tasks, and workflow of the interface.

Lessons from the immediate past and glimpses of future theories

Don Norman and the user-centered design school of thought are the right choices to approach current design discourse and practices.

But there are a lot of ideas in media theory and even semiotics that are hard to miss.

In his first publications, McLuhan analyses pop culture, its influence, and rhetoric in society. But with *The Gutenberg Galaxy*, his attention pointed toward how new technologies change our minds and culture.

Oral language, manuscript culture, printing press, movies, books, newspapers, TV, cars, planes, and computers... were some of the new technologies he addressed.

Some of his proposals could be outdated but not his ways and methods.

After McLuhan, we had Umberto Eco and Roland Barthes. Both wrote about media culture as McLuhan did. Barthes didn't meet the internet. Eco did and had a very pessimistic — even apocalyptic — vision about it.

Anyway, we used work written in the decade of the 1960s by McLuhan to explain what was happening in the 1990s.

We are using the work written in the 2010s' decade by Norman to explain what is happening in the 2020s.

It would be interesting to know what school of thought we are going to use to explain the 2030s decade and beyond.

(Published on Jan 16, 2020, in Concepts Against Reality)

38

6

You know Norman doors, but what about Norman washer-dryers?

Designing simple objects is easy. The challenge is with complex devices

Every user experience designer has read Don Norman's book, *The Design of Everyday Things* or at least has heard about the Norman doors.[28]

A door is a simple and common object that doesn't need an explanation of how to use it and it shouldn't be difficult to use it too. Although, you find a lot of doors that are confusing because you don't know if you have to pull, push, slide or turn.

How can such a simple thing as a door be so confusing?

---

[28] "*The Design of Everyday Things.*" In *Wikipedia*, December 21, 2022. https://en.wikipedia.org/w/index.php?title=The_Design_of_Everyday_Things&oldid=1128768800.

A door would seem to be about as simple a device as possible. There is not much you can do to a door: you can open it or shut it. — Don Norman

Don Norman doesn't give visual examples in his book to illustrate his point and I'm not going to do that either. But if you want them, some people like to collect them.[29]

Norman doors are easy to detect and easy to make fun of. That's why they are so popular. They are too obvious even for a child.

But the father of user experience design gives another example in his book that I found far more interesting: the washer-dryer machines.

What is a Norman washer-dryer?

Don Norman says that a door is a simple object so to have the two characteristics of good design — discoverability and understanding — in it shouldn't be a problem.

And he's right. But after you talk about Norman doors with your non-designer colleagues or student designers — and even some experienced designers — you will find that the characteristics of good design are not as easy as designing a door.

Most of our everyday things are complex and are becoming more complex with new technologies: stoves, washing ma-

---

[29] normandoors. "Norman Doors." Tumblr. A Norman Door is a door whose design tells the person to do the opposite of what they're actually supposed to do. It is an example of something which is badly designed, which confuses the user. This... Accessed March 23, 2023. https://normandoors.tumblr.com/.

chines, audio and television sets, mobile phones...

We can argue that the complexity of some of these new objects is always necessary, but that's for another story.

Complex devices require the aid of manuals or personal training. The discoverability and understanding are not as obvious as a simple object like a door.

The example Don Norman gives in his book for complex objects is a "fancy new Italian washer-dryer combination, with super-duper multi-symbol controls" he found at some friend's home.

You may feel identified with the husband who avoids the machine — although he is an engineering psychologist — or with the wife who uses only one of the configuration sets and ignores the rest.

Norman checked the manual of the artifact just to see that it was as confusing as the device.

We find more washer-dryer machines in our daily lives than doors.

A popular software application like Microsoft Office Word is a good example or a washer-dryer machine. Most of the users are like the husband or the wife in Norman's story.

Or the user avoids most of the menus and functions and tries to rest in the commodity of the templates, or s/he learns how to use the most basic features and keeps sticking to them.

The design of everyday complex things

Don't be fooled by the complexity of an object. It should be easy to use too.

• "You can't make it more simply because it's a complex

device"
- "This is a high piece of technology with a longer learning curve".
- "More advanced technology needs more advanced users".
- "It's a rule that 95% of the people only use the 5% of the functions".

You may find these excuses alike when talking about the design of complex objects. None of them are right.

As I said, complex devices may require the aid of manuals or personal training. But that doesn't have to be a pretext to do complex and unusable designs.

At some moments in my career, I have worked as a technical writer and as a technical trainer. Sometimes a bad design pretends to be solved with the instruction manual or with training. But when the design is bad, the discoverability and understanding of errors make themselves more evident in the instructions or in the training—the contradictions emerge.

How to compose music for an orchestra

How to accomplish simplicity in a complex device? Simple elements form complex things.

Good design rules and principles apply to any kind of device. You just need to realize that when you compose music for an orchestra, every instrument has different sheet music.

With complex experiences, you may have multiple user journeys, but each has to be simple. Or with complex interfaces, you may have multiple user flows, but each has to be simple too.

As I like to say when talking about complex and simple

devices, a door is a simple device for a more complex system — a building. And even a door has simpler parts: lock, panels, casing, jamb, hinges...

A washer-dryer is a very useful object at home and its discoverability and understanding characteristics as a whole might not be as easy as a door. But the particular steps to put a couple of jeans in to wash or dry might be very easy.

The Norman washer-dryer machine is the true challenge a user experience o product designer faces to accomplish her or his work.

How do you accomplish that challenge?

(Published on Feb 17, 2020, on Medium)

7

How to use the Norman door as a conceptual framework

The question you have to ask about any design is: what if this was a door?

Since I read the book by Don Norman, *The Design of Everyday Things,* the example of the doors in the first chapters works as a mind tool in my brain. I'm always comparing any product or user experience with a door.

This is an attempt to build a conceptual framework from that way of thinking. You probably do the same comparison without explicitly thinking about it. Or you may just get some research and design ideas for your next project.

What is a conceptual framework?

A conceptual framework is like a metaphor but with steroids. We usually use metaphors to understand and explain our world. But metaphors can be too imaginative, fantastic, and even poetic to work with.[30]

But when you complement a metaphor with analytical thinking you can build a conceptual framework.

- Identify the elements of the metaphor to get concepts.
- Identify the context of the metaphor to get categories.
- Identify what the metaphor represents, to get deductions.
- Organizing the elements, their relations, and interactions to frame them.
- Applying them to understand and reorganize new realities.

In science and research, you call them conceptual frameworks. For more regular and common use, you usually call them 'mental models'.[31] But in the context of user experience design, 'mental model' means 'mental representations',[32] so I prefer 'conceptual framework' to avoid confusion.

A good example of a conceptual framework is the way we usually understand the business, marketing, or sales competition using the reference of sports. For instance, we talk about rivals, teams, goals, strategies, tactics, motivation, defense, attack,

---

[30] "Conceptual Framework." In *Wikipedia*, February 19, 2023. https://en.wiki pedia.org/w/index.php?title=Conceptual_framework&oldid=1140298133.

[31] "Mental Model." In *Wikipedia*, March 15, 2023. https://en.wikipedia.org/ w/index.php?title=Mental_model&oldid=1144827495.

[32] "Mental Representation." In *Wikipedia*, March 22, 2023. https://en.wikipe dia.org/w/index.php?title=Mental_representation&oldid=1146020569.

front line, bank, coach, etc. We articulate these concepts to understand and organize our business or company.

We say in a business meeting: "Imagine we are playing football..."

Let's see which are the elements and context in a Norman door to abstract and organize them.

The metaphor of the Norman door

> *The design of the door should indicate how to work it without any need for signs, certainly without any need for trial and error.* — Don Norman, The Design of Everyday Things

Don Norman, the father of user experience design, uses a door as an example of bad design in his book *The Design of Everyday Things* — if you have to explain how to use a door it's not well designed. Now it's a designer's reference to explain a bad design.

I'm not going to stop by the details. Let's find the elements to build the conceptual framework.

- the door is the object of design
- it's an object for an ordinary user
- the user needs to use it
- the user can open or shut it
- the design should communicate how to use it, with no labels, no trial or error.
- the user easily finds out how to use it
- the user easily understands what it is and its parts

46

Let's add user needs to expand the framework:

· the door is a medium — a tool — for a major goal
· the major goal is on the mind of the user, not the door
· when achieving his goal, the user will not remember the door

And the context:

· a door is a common object of everyday use
· a door is a simple device

The Norman door as a conceptual framework

The question you have to ask about any design is: if this object was a door, would it be a Norman door?

Using the Norman door as an analogy or a model, we have to answer the following questions:

1. What is the object that works like a door? Are you going to analyze just a part of the object? Only one interface? Are you defining well the object?
2. How does the user define the object?
3. You know what makes a door a door? What makes the new object its kind of object? Can you identify other objects in the same category?
4. Does the user know what makes the object that kind of object? Is this something s/he has to find out?
5. Who is the common user for this object? How common? Think about the most common user.
6. How does the user use the other objects in the cate-

gory? What are the well-designed objects in the category? Which are the bad ones? Why?

7. Why does the user need to use the object? Does s/he have an alternative?

8. Is the object the major goal for the user or just a medium — tool, or container? What is the major goal?

9. In a few words, what can the user do with the object? Look not just for the more probable uses but the possible uses.

10. Does the user need additional instructions on how to use the object? Is it a straightforward process? How many instructions?

11. Can the user find out by herself or himself how to use it? Is everything s/he needs at hand, in plain sight?

Let's see these questions in a diagram. For each question, there is an answer delimiting the object and the point of view of the user. And as an example, imagine the product is the first iPhone by Apple.

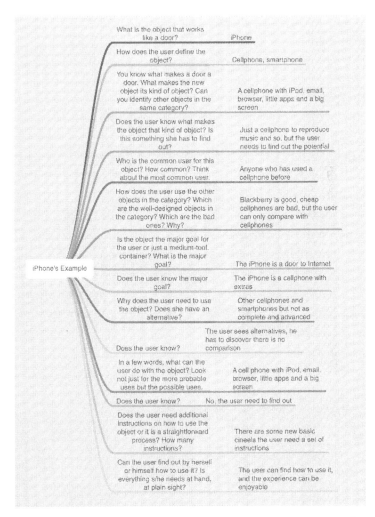

As you can see, there is a very big difference between what the object is and the expectations of the user.

That doesn't mean that the first iPhone was going to be a Norman door — in this example, we know it was a success — but we have to understand that the design of an object like the

49

iPhone needs to be approached by its parts.

Simple objects and complex objects

The Norman door framework can be used for simple things. But, if you have a complex one, you can use it to separate the object into its parts.

Every object has parts. Complex objects can be seen as a system with elements interconnected. A door is part of a building. A lock is part of a door.

To resolve a complex problem you divide the problem into parts. To design a complex object you divide it into parts.

Every part of a complex object is a Norman door to which you can apply this framework.

Back to our example, the iPhone as a whole can be a Norman door. We have to think about a complex object as a building, and then consider the doors.

If an iPhone is a building, the cell phone part of it is a door. It has other parts, but we think of them one by one. So, in this conceptual framework, we have to design a very good user experience with the cellphone — or the Phone app.

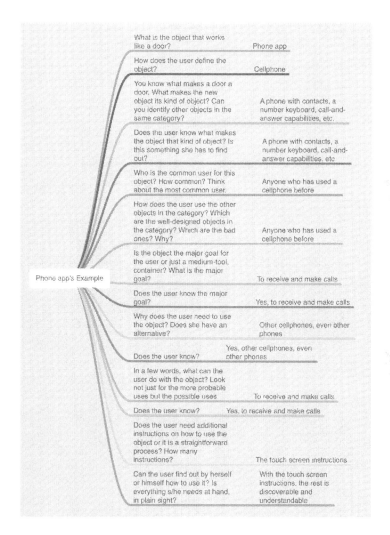

As you can see, now we have a better relationship between the user and the Phone app. The Phone app is not a Norman door.

Every part of a more complex device must be designed with the characteristics of a good design.

This is the reason that facilitated the adoption of a complex device like the iPhone: as a whole was a challenge for the user, but every part was as simple as a door.

As I said, the use of the conceptual framework of the Norman door it's very intuitive for me. I don't answer the questions on the table every time I need to analyze an object.

But it works very well when I try to explain a design element to a developer, for example. "Imagine this is a door..."

What do you think? Does this work for you?

(Published on Feb 18, 2020, in UX Collective)

II

On UX designing and thinking

8

The best type of user you want for your app

This kind of user will make a hole where you built a wall

So, you have finished the last ultimate user experience design. Your ideas have materialized into an app or service. You have the elements, the fonts, colors, menus, buttons... everything according to the functions defined. You have done your research. You have perfectly studied the user flow or user journey and the user personas. Everything is in place.

Most of your users are happy with most of the functionalities and design of the app. But there is a very special group of users that weren't reflected in the research because there isn't research that can get them.

This special kind of user not just likes and wants very specific tools or configurations — you already have thought about that kind of user — but this doesn't accept a "no" or "that isn't possible to do it" for an answer. We can call them hackers.

No, I'm not talking about security or privacy. Not the kind of hacker that tries to break a system to take advantage of it. Not all thieves are hackers and not all hackers are thieves. Let me try to define a hacker as a user in a broader sense.

You may think that good design or development has to be anti-hacking, meaning that the user doesn't have to hack a design to use it. Wrong.

What does a hacker do? A hacker is going to check every menu, every corner of your app or service. Probably before the hacker uses it. And then, after some minutes of finally working on it, the hacker's going to need a special configuration. It can be a change in the font face or the font size. Or it can be in the types of files you can export. Perhaps an interface to connect to another app or service. They are going to send you an email asking for your API access. Whatever it is, if the hacker doesn't find how to change it, the hacker is going to start a quest to accomplish it.

> *"It is hard to write a simple definition of something as varied as hacking, but I think what these activities have in common is playfulness, cleverness, and exploration. Thus, hacking means exploring the limits of what is possible, in a spirit of playful cleverness. Activities that display playful cleverness have 'hack value'."—Richard Stallman, On Hacking[33]*

As I said, I'm not talking about the kind of hacker that steals passwords or breaks the security of servers. Neither I'm

---

[33] "On Hacking - Richard Stallman." Accessed March 15, 2023. https://stallman.org/articles/on-hacking.html.

talking about geeks with professional knowledge and particular requirements. By hackers I mean the kind of user that likes to do extra configurations and is good at understanding how a system or a machine works and is capable of making changes.

> "In general, **hackers are problem solvers**. Hackers are scrappy. Hackers express themselves with computer code and use their skills to solve problems." —Chris Castiglione at Hacker Noon[34]

Car customizers

If you design cars, you will find that there is a special kind of user that loves to customize her or his vehicles.[35] They swap motors, change the painting, and add their special styling with accessories. They are the equivalent of the hacker users I'm talking about.

Not all their customizations are for styling purposes. Some of them update the security requirements of old cars to the ones used today.

They have groups, communities, awards... They share tutorials, tips, recommendations... They have their own slang and terminology...

Sound familiar? They are hackers from the pre-internet and digitalization era.

---

[34] "The Secret Hacker Code | HackerNoon." Accessed March 15, 2023. https://hackernoon.com/the-secret-hacker-code-974bc55af261.

[35] "Custom Car." In *Wikipedia*, March 12, 2023. https://en.wikipedia.org/w/index.php?title=Custom_car&oldid=1144201326.

What should you do?

You always have to give space to hackers. Call them advanced users, advanced settings, or, as they prefer, API, internal configurations, scripts, macros...

For Google Chrome there are extensions and there is chrome://flags, where you can tweak the configuration or text some features. iOS bought an app that automates tasks, called *Shortcuts*. Apps for developers like Github have desktop apps you can use through the graphic interface, just click with your cursor. But they also have a Github CLI for those who prefer to work in the terminal. In any operating system, you can access the command-line interface. Autocad has scripting capabilities and in Figma, you can install or even develop plugins.

Other apps and services like Jekyll and WordPress try to create communities or forums where users can share experiences and give space to advanced users to share tips and hacks. Some apps, especially open-source apps, depend entirely on the user's communities, and the communities of the hackers or advanced users.

In the case of the browser tabs

For instance, the use of multiple tabs in browsers like Google Chrome has become excessive and people have too many tabs open at the same time. Each tab consumes memory and resources. One developer created a great extension for that called *The Great Suspender*. After a few minutes of not using a tab, the extension discards the content, keeping the URL and cache in memory. When you return to the tab, the extension reloads the content. This way you can make the browser faster.

The Chrome developer's team took that into consideration and implemented the same function. First as a "flag" for advanced users, and then natively in the browser. They even had a chat with the creator of the extension.[36]

Curiously, there is no option now. Chrome discards the tabs you are not using automatically. No questions asked, no customization options. Guess what! Now, there is a new extension to disable automatic tab discarding.[37] The hackers, again.

The case of the colorless interface

There is a hack that has become a trend, first in geek's forums but now you find it even in main newspapers articles. For that, you change the screen of your smartphone from the default color interface to a grayscaled one. The reason? There is the hypothesis that if you quit the color attractiveness of your screen you use it less. Now that the tech community is talking about cellphone addiction, this is one hack you can try to overcome such addiction.

But of course, no smartphone designer thought about this when designing it. Some users — hackers — found that in the accessibility configuration, there is an option to originally do that for people with visual impairment.

---

[36] Chrome Developers. "Tab Discarding in Chrome - A Memory-Saving Experiment." Accessed March 15, 2023. https://developer.chrome.com/blog/tab-discarding/.

[37] "Disable Automatic Tab Discarding." Accessed March 15, 2023. https://chrome.google.com/webstore/detail/disable-automatic-tab-dis/dnhngfnfolbmhgealdpolmhimnoliiok.

Building doors

You have to give an option to hackers. Maybe not at the beginning of your product launch but keep that on the roadmap. Gmail was very minimalist and without too many features to customize at the beginning. They added advanced preferences and "Labs" later on. Today there are a lot of extensions to maximize their use.

> *"What they had in common was mainly love of excellence and programming. They wanted to make their programs that they used be as good as they could. They also wanted to make them do neat things. They wanted to be able to do something in a more exciting way than anyone believed possible and show 'Look how wonderful this is. I bet you didn't believe this could be done.'"* —Richard Stallman in the documentary Hackers —Wizards of the Electronic Age[38]

It's difficult to respond to the hackers' requirements. But this kind of user is the same that can give you great ideas to add or change in your app or service.

You can always keep your basic interface for your general use and leave the space for modifications in a special tab, menu, or link. Don't worry, the hackers don't need to have it in plain sight. They may even like to find it by themselves like easter eggs in software or cheat codes in games.

When you, a designer, developer, or engineer, use an app or

---

[38] "Hackers Video," November 29, 2022. https://web.archive.org/web/20221 129183437/http://www.handtap.com/hackers/.

service and think about what you would want differently and even maybe change some things in it, you are being a hacker.

So, don't hate hackers. Learn to love them. They are like us. They dedicate extra time to your app or service. They are the best users because they have learned how things work.

If your design is hacked, redesign it. Hackers find holes where designers build walls. Don't try to fill the holes. Built a door instead.

(Published on Apr 10, 2020, in UX Collective)

9

Designers propose, users dispose

Copy-pasting, zapping, surfing, photoshopping, googling, taking selfies: when the user reuses the user experience

> *In any human network, language is the main intermediary. It's the protocol that all the nodes in a network use to interface with each other.* — *James Currier*[39]

Before computers became a commercial success, our reference for them was science fiction. Science fiction gave us intuition about our future with computers: *I, Robot, Star Trek, Star Wars...* you name it.

Calculators, androids, speaking assistants, hand-held com-

---

[39] NFX. "The Network Effects Manual: 16 Different Network Effects (and Counting)," June 25, 2021. https://www.nfx.com/post/network-effects-manual.

puters, dashboards on screens, translators...

But in no science fiction was a prediction on copy-paste, web surfing, photoshopping, googling, or taking selfies.

These are some of the practices that have become embedded not just in our daily use of gadgets and applications but in our culture and our daily use of words.

The commands copy, cut and paste are default in any operative system or app. But they are also part of the way we think. If someone tells you she or he has to capture the text you email her or email him, you know this person is from another planet. On this planet, everybody knows copy-pasting exists.

Knowledge is power

Throughout history, the conqueror imposes its language over the conquered. Latin was the language of the Roman Empire. Spanish disappeared from native languages in New Spain.

Power relationships in society are expressed through language and practices. Power is linked to the formation of discourse.

These are the ideas of Michel Foucault, French philosopher, and author of books like *The Order of Things, Archeology of Knowledge,* and *The Discourse On Language.*

Knowledge is power too, and language is the key to closing it or opening it. The Greek language survived and even influenced Latin because of the Greek Culture and what we inherit from it: alphabet, Olympics, trial by jury, Philosophy, Physics, democracy, mathematics, Euclid geometry, Pedagogy...

Besides politics and war, we have experienced this in our daily life. Tribes, gangs, and clubs keep a set of coded words and practices called slang. You are part of the group when you understand them and talk like them. That's when you know the code.

When new knowledge is acquired, words, phrases, and sentences become concepts, declarations, and statements.

> *As jargon gets adopted by more and more people, it becomes more valuable to all the other users. —James Currier*[40]

Jargon and technical terms are protocols in any knowledge domain. To learn about a new topic, vocabulary, and glossaries are the tactical points to get into it.

User experiences and practices

Practices, as Foucault calls them, are these new behaviors, activities, or events that become rituals, customs, and even rules. That's what constitutes culture.

For example, the theater in the Greek culture—in the dramatic sense of the word—came from ancient cults, chorus songs, and a society with a high value on the spoken word and storytelling.

These practices went from activities—tragedy, drama, comedy—to buildings—the space of representation—and finally to art—as structured knowledge.

Theatre was a completely new practice with its own language, therefore a new knowledge and a new power.

---

[40] NFX. "The Network Effects Manual: 16 Different Network Effects (and Counting)," June 25, 2021. https://www.nfx.com/post/network-effects-manual.

In this sense, user experiences are practices. The interface is a language, an intermediate between the practice and the user. Let's use copy and paste as an example.

Imagine you are Larry Tesler, the inventor of the copy-paste command. First, as a designer or developer, you resolve a user's problem with a system to grab data, store it for later use, and then print it or transport it to another place. Then, you think in an interface — a language — to call the command: copy and paste.[41]

These words look like common words — like a square button looks like a common square — but they are not. They are the keys to a door, words that do things, and interfaces.

But after the user learns to use the interface, there is an appropriation process where the user takes the words or interface as her/his own.

Copy-paste — the interface — becomes an experience. You don't teach a new employee how to copy-paste. As I said below, if you don't know what copy-paste is, you are not from this planet, or from this culture. You have no power.

Category design as new practices

A good marketing example of how a new practice creates a new language is category design.

In the ancient Greek's example, theatre is a product and a user experience in a new art category, next to music, dance, or sculpture.

In the current world, you design or redesign objects or expe-

---

[41] "Larry Tesler." In *Wikipedia*, March 5, 2023. https://en.wikipedia.org/w/index.php?title=Larry_Tesler&oldid=1143093873.

riences for a category: watches, chairs, spreadsheet programs, cinema complexes, buildings... The category exists, you design something within the category.

But there is category design. You design an object or an experience without category. In this case, you practically design the category itself. The iPhone created the category of smartphones. Netflix created the category of video streaming. Uber or Airbnb are other typical examples.

Both, iPhone and Netflix were in a category at the beginning — cellphones and video streaming. But the particularities of their design separate them from the others in the category to build a category for themselves — smartphones and streaming subscription-based movies and TV series.

Categories are not isolated. They inherit characteristics from their ancestors or share qualities with their neighbors.

Uber looks like a taxi business, Airbnb looks like a hosting business. We try to put these new products or experiences in old categories just to understand them. But they are a category by themselves.

When a new category emerges it brings new interactions with its users. Sometimes the interactions are completely original. And most of the time the new behavior can't be anticipated for the creator or designer of the new category. It's almost impossible to do it.

These new behaviors are what Foucault calls practices.

Zapping

New practices and the new words that define them are not exclusive to our modern digital life.

Back in the nineteen-seventies, to change the channel on

the TV set at home, you had to stand up and turn the dial on the device. There were not too many channels to choose from anyway.

The wired remote control was commercially available at the end of the seventies but was rapidly substituted by the wireless remote control in most of the new TVs from the nineteen-eighties.

A new behavior emerged in parallel with a wider offer of cable and satellite TV channels: zapping or channel surfing.

Zapping was a completely new phenomenon. The audience, especially people watching TV alone, spend significant minutes changing from one channel to another hoping to find a program to watch.

I can write several paragraphs about it, but just let me say that this user experience was an interaction with the TV by itself. You couldn't define what channel or program the audience was watching at a given moment because of the constant surfing. It was a way in which the users created or edited their own content.

This behavior persists throughout our days. Zapping started as an interface but now it is an experience.

Web surfing

Similar to zapping, with the arrival of the World Wide Web, surfing and browsing emerged. It is difficult to surf between articles in magazines or chapters within books, but when the information is in a digital form, hyperlinked and on a network, going from one node to another takes a click.

Photoshopping

Photoshop wasn't the first app used to alter, edit or modify a picture. But as a product, it imposed a practice. You might not use Photoshop to photoshop a photo.

The understanding of this practice is embedded in our culture as copying and pasting, but the consequences are far bigger. In a strict sense, photography was never the reality, but for general uses, a photograph had this aura of authenticity. Today with the photoshopping culture, nobody believes that anymore.

"Just google it!"

Searching the Internet was a necessity along with its invention, but Google brought the indexing of full-text pages, a reliable algorithm to show relevant results, and fast response to inquiries.

The company took full advantage of capturing and registering the words and phrases used for searching to improve the experience until reaching the point of allowing asking questions written almost like natural language.

Googling is not just a new behavior but probably a new paradigm for our culture and society. As happened with writing and the printing press, it is even changing the way humans acquire, process, and consult information.

Taking selfies

The self-photo shoot was practically born with photography itself. And more recently, the Japanese used to adopt the practice before our Western culture. But as a particular and mass-adopted behavior, it emerged with the use of cameras in smartphones until the beginning of the century and was heavily propelled by the iPhone 4.

The front camera was the interface for a new experience called taking selfies. But now taking selfies is the experience itself.

The user strikes back

the role played by users can never be underestimated.—
Carlos A. Scolari[42]

Something interesting to add. No designer could imagine what the user was going to do with zapping, copy-pasting, photoshopping, surfing, googling, or taking selfies. The user practice overcomes the intention of the interface.

For instance, zapping was a tool to go from one channel to another, but the user transformed it into a way to watch TV.

As Carlos A. Scolari points out, "tactics are the resource of the weak to counteract the strategy of the strong, then it is pertinent to speak of 'user tactics' when deviant or unforeseen uses are implemented".[43]

---

[42] Scolari, Carlos A. "Ninth Law of the Interface: Interfaces Are Political." Medium, February 19, 2020. https://uxdesign.cc/ninth-law-of-the-interface-the-design-and-use-of-an-interface-are-political-practices-8f1fa5e6c2ae.

[43] Scolari, Carlos A. "Ninth Law of the Interface: Interfaces Are Political." Medium, February 19, 2020. https://uxdesign.cc/ninth-law-of-the-interface-the-design-and-use-of-an-interface-are-political-practices-8f1fa5e6c2ae.

Designer proposes...

As a designer, you never know how the user is going to adopt the interactions of experiences you propose. That is why there is no final product but constant iterations.

There is a continuous flow between the experience, the user, and the interface that goes beyond the product. The user uses but also reuses. The designer proposes, user disposes.

UX design, but especially UX writing, can be very powerful. Power as in politics, not just as in tooling.

(Published on Feb 26, 2020, in UX Collective)

10

To surprise or not to surprise your users

Lessons learned from a startled fruit fly

Do you want to startle your users? Yes and no. It depends. Maybe a little. Maybe sometimes. There are principles. But, they are to be broken, right?

The answer could be in the fruit flies.

But first, let's remember the principle of least astonishment or least surprise which in simple words says, don't unnecessarily surprise the users.[44] Or, don't try to redesign what it is already designed.

Everybody knows how to open a door. You don't redesign a door by changing the basic principles of what a door is and how it is used. You can change the color, the surface, the patterns

---

[44] Bloch, Joshua. *How to Design a Good API and Why It Matters.* Association for Computing Machinery, 2006. http://portal.acm.org/citation.cfm?id=1176 622.

or motives, or the images on the door.

But if your design or redesign makes the user stop the previous flow and knowledge using a door, something is wrong with the design. No matter how cool your design looks, nobody is going to learn how to use a door because you change it.

Your design doesn't have to startle your user.

That's clear and logical, right?

Every rule has an exception

Well, but, in a world where you want to be distinguished from others, you want to get attention. You want to design something that is different from the rest.

And besides, innovation surprises.

Your design heroes do that all the time.[45] First, they got rid of the floppy drive unit from the iMac. Then, they got rid of the DVD unit. And the ethernet port. and the USB port.

Users were startled by any of those changes, for sure.

Or in the iPhone, they removed all the buttons to leave the minimum of them, practically, just the home button. And they removed the antenna. And the audio jack.

Then, they removed the home button too.

Again, every time, the users were startled by those changes.

> *I actually think the path of holding onto features that have been effective, the path of holding onto those whatever the cost, is a path that leads to failure.* —Jony

---

[45] Paste Magazine. "5 Controversial Technology Choices That Apple Was Right About." Accessed March 16, 2023. https://www.pastemagazine.com/tech/apple/5-controversial-apple-innovations-that-it-was-righ.

Ive[46]

Well, it seems that the principle of least astonishment doesn't apply to your design heroes. They startle the users, they change the user flow, and they innovate.

In fact, they get more users because of that!

So, to surprise or not to surprise your users? That is the question.

The "wow" moment

There is a simple way to resolve this. You reserve the "wow" moments for the interactions that are really important and your users already want.

It's like when you ride a rollercoaster. You are there because you want to be surprised by the ride, the curves, and the falls… but you want to arrive at your seat securely, and you want to leave your seat securely too.

In a camera app, for example, you usually expect that the menu and buttons are going to be standard. You want to take a photo, that's all. So, the designer doesn't mess with the camera itself. You open, you see, you choose options, and you shoot.

The "wow" moment is reserved when you have the option to choose a filter, for example. Those filters and how you are going to use them are where the designers have to put their efforts.

You get surprised by the different options of filters, their

[46] Time. "Apple's Jony Ive Talks to TIME About Designing the IPhone X," November 16, 2017. https://time.com/5025887/apple-jony-ive-iphone-x/.

originality, etc.

But what happens when the design is going to change an expected behavior? What happens when you take off the expected physical keyboard from a cellphone like the Blackberry and you change it for a screen, like the iPhone?

Lessons learned from a startled fruit fly

I just read that scientists proved that the neurochemical involved when some living beings are startled is serotonin. Well, at least in the fruit fly.[47]

Any change in the environment causes a release of serotonin in the brain of the fruit fly. Serotonin is the neurotransmitter that makes us awake, among other things.

During the day, your brain accumulates melatonin. When there is too much melatonin, you start to feel sleepy.

When you go to sleep the levels of melatonin decrease and the levels of serotonin start to increase. When there is too much serotonin, you start to wake up.

It looks like serotonin is also released when the brain and body perceive a change in the environment. A rapid release. Which sounds logical, because you need to wake up and be ready for a fight or flight.

But, for a moment, you are paralyzed. Well, the fruit fly for sure. But it seems that we can apply the same to us and other mammals. What paralyzes you is serotonin, the same neurochemical that wakes you up.

---

[47] ScienceDaily. "Why Do We Freeze When Startled? New Study in Flies Points to Serotonin." Accessed March 16, 2023. https://www.sciencedaily.com/releases/2019/11/191127161446.htm.

Do you remember the deer-in-the-headlights reflex? If you headlight a deer in the dark, the deer is going to freeze. Same principle.

Thanks to that serotonin release, we have survived. It's a good thing. Any change in the environment could be a danger. And there is no space for speculation. We have to stop. If we are running, walking, eating, drinking, hunting, or fishing... we have to stop immediately.

What is important here is what happens next. After being startled we need security. The fruit flies, and we, humans, stop or freeze just in order to look for security.

> *Imagine sitting in your living room with your family and—all of a sudden—the lights go out, or the ground begins to shake. Your response, and that of your family, will be the same: You will stop, freeze and then move to safety.—Richard Mann, PhD[48]*

Every time you startle your users for a reason, you have to give them security immediately after that.

Let's see the case with the keyboard.

Imagine it's 2007 year. You have the first iPhone in your hands. You receive a text message like you used to receive on your old phone. You don't have a keyboard like you used to have in that Blackberry or Nokia. You open the message and you may be startled because you don't see the keyboard to write an answer. But as soon as you start reading, the keyboard is

---

[48] ScienceDaily. "Why Do We Freeze When Startled? New Study in Flies Points to Serotonin." Accessed March 16, 2023. https://www.sciencedaily.com/releases/2019/11/191127161446.htm.

there, on the screen. You can write back.

After startling your users, you give them their security back.

And you give them something in exchange for that little and brief discomfort: a big and lovely screen.

Remember

So, to startle or not to startle your users? I think we can learn some things from the fruit fly.

1. You don't change the expected user flow.
2. You reserve the surprises or "wow" moments and place them where the user expects them.
3. But if you are going to startle the users by changing their usual flow, you must give them security immediately after that.
4. And, any modification in the user's flow has to give them something in exchange: a nice and lovely improvement.

(Published on Dec 9, 2019, in UX Collective)

11

Frictionless experiences make us fragile

Or the trend to find a note-taking app that takes notes for you

The easy way

These days, it looks like we are living in the quest to design and build the ultimate frictionless experience. From boarding an airplane to configuring an app, through shopping online or playing music, everything seems to be around getting a frictionless experience.

This trend can go to extremes. In the area of note-taking apps, for example, I see requests from users that want a simple button not only to capture all the highlights from their ebook readers but to get all the transcripts from the podcasts they listen to, previously letting them select their favorite time stamps.

In other words, these days almost everybody wants to avoid

using a note-taking app to take notes. "Why take notes in a note-taking app if I can find an app to do it for me?", seems to be the user story here.

Surprisingly, after they want all those notes imported — sometimes they use the word "synced" — they figure out that they want to remember all that stuff because the users notice that they forget the notes very easily, so they request a spaced repetition system or automatic flashcards to remember and memorize all those notes.

The users expect to have all these note-taking functions without having to type anything.

Curiously, if you write down by handwriting or typing your notes, you can remember them better — no need for another memory method.

(If you want a frictionless link to the scientific reference of handwriting and learning you are not going to get it here; go, do your own research.)

Experience and friction

If you want to avoid the friction of reading more let me state clearly what I think about the ultimate frictionless experience so you can decide whether to keep reading or not.

Frictionless experiences make us fragile.

Experience is everything except frictionless. And learning? There is no learning by osmosis or transmissionism—we only can learn by experience.

Even when we are learning about abstract concepts like mathematics, the definitions are not enough—we need to demonstrate, calculate, graph, write down the equation, and do the math!

That's why a mathematician needs to use the blackboard or the notebook: that's the doing of thinking.

For example, when we try to give detailed instructions to children about a task, we usually make the task harder to follow. Being overprotective of our children can hurt them more than help them.

There are no instruction manuals for climbing trees.

Paraphrasing Gary Klein (*Sources of Power, The Power of Intuition*), an excess of procedures makes us fragile because makes us think about the procedure first and in the experience later.

When you don't have a strict procedure, you are giving space to uncertainty, so you get ready for it. But when you follow a strict procedure you are just pretending you are in control which makes you a prey of uncertainty.

If we want to learn from experience — or live a whole experience in general —, we need surprise in it, uncertainty, challenge, toughness, force, and reinforcement, because just when we get over these obstacles, we can feel the pleasure of finishing a task. And is in that moment that a memory — a new path in our mind — can emerge.

So, we learn, we grow, we gain, and we became stronger.

Friction and frictionless experiences

Do you want to know about all the frictionless experiences I've had? I don't remember them. They didn't leave a footprint in my memory.

On the other hand, I consider myself an advanced user of Excel. I learned it in an era without the internet, or at least, without Youtube or extended tutorials.

I had my initiation rite going through trial and error, searching for the right formula, thinking about combinations, questioning if the spreadsheet could do what I wanted, and of course, in the end, having the pleasure of getting a file working as I wanted.

I can tell you if you want to learn Excel your experience is going to be everything but frictionless.

Unless you look for the answer to your question in Google, find a tutorial with code included, copy and paste it on your spreadsheet, make little modifications, and get the solution working almost without friction. Because in that case, I can assure you, you are not going to learn Excel.

The funny thing, the next time you're going to have the same problem, you are going to walk the same steps without noticing. Maybe after you finish, you are going to have a little *deja vu* and say, "I think I have done this before".

Yes, a frictionless experience makes us fragile.

The right amount and the right kind

Of course, there is useless friction, friction that doesn't help the experience. And also, there is friction that can be more challenging, ergo, better for plenty of experience and learning.

You can try to design that for an experience. But sometimes you just create a tool or method that is useful *per se*. The users have to figure out the rest by themselves. That's the case with carpentry tools or programming languages.

Friction in experiences—the right amount and the right kind—can make us less fragile, more robust, and even the opposite of fragile, antifragile. To gain and grow.

FRICTIONLESS EXPERIENCES MAKE US FRAGILE

(Published on Aug 17, 2021, on Medium)

12

Why information alone won't help you improve your game anymore?

How to use experience to create experience

It may seem obvious, but as a user experience designer or UX—as much as any designer, producer, or creator—you shouldn't rely only on data and information to make decisions, no matter if it comes from quantitative or qualitative research.

When I was a child I remember an interview on TV with the coach of one of my favorite sports teams. In that interview, he explained how important it was to record on film the games to analyze them later.

First, I imagined how cool it would be to watch again and again the moves and plays catching errors in a game to improve the strategies. At that time, you didn't have a VCR at home yet, so to have a film camera and a way to watch the repetitions was like science fiction to me.

Yes, I'm this old.

But later on, I thought that every team in the league should have the same resources for a film camera to analyze the games. So, what was the advantage?

There is no secret formula

Every time you take a piece of advice or apply a new marketing or design method or technique you must take into consideration that your competition is doing the same.

There are no secret strategies to get more followers, readers, online sales, better SEO, more effective designs, or whatever you or your business need.

And if someone tells you that has a secret to achieving success in a market, take into account that a business secret is always a product itself. Sooner or later is going to stop being a secret.

Let me say it like this. When everybody is playing the same playbook, there is no advantage in using it. The playbook becomes a standard or a basic business handbook.

"The secret to writing a good headline"

A very good example is how to write headlines to attract readers. No matter the content you use to convert views into readers, readers into users, and users into customers, there is already a playbook for that.

Blogs, infographics, case studies, videos, white papers, social media posts... any of these need a headline. What does the playbook tell us about it?

- Use lists and include numbers, how-tos, or questions.
- Mix words that convey emotions and power.

- Use common words combined with technical ones.
- Not too short, not too wordy.
- Don't forget attractive adjectives.
- Good call-to-action words would be nice.
- Etcetera.

It's so easy to simply google "how to write headlines to attract... " and have very good tips and examples for that. There are even headline analyzers and headline generators to test yours, free for all.

So, if everybody is writing the same type of headlines, what is the advantage?

This is just an example, but let's see an app and service to get more sales. Salesforce is a good case. The business that used Salesforce fifteen years ago had an advantage over the competition, just until the competition started to use this CRM or a similar one.

If you don't like Salesforce or it's too expensive, you just have to google "Salesforce vs..." or "Salesforce alternatives" to find a CRM for you.

Have you started using Figma to take advantage of its features? Your competition too. And the other design apps have started to copy those new features from Figma also.

What is your competitive advantage?

You have heard that information creates knowledge. But, what happens when information is available to anyone? The competition is harder.

Where can you take advantage? The advantage is no longer in data, information, or knowledge. Well, at least not in the knowledge that comes from information.

The advantage is in the experience. Or, if you prefer, in the knowledge that comes from experience.

Remember I told you you have to practice what you preach?

Experience can't be learned by reading or watching. Experience can't go from one brain to another, or from one computer to another.

The only way to get experience is by doing things.

And I'm talking about *your* experience, not the experience you are designing for others.

The best example of this is the way you learn to ride a bike. You can't learn how to ride a bike by reading a book or watching a youtube video. No one can give you the secret of riding a bike and keeping it in your brain. The only way to learn how to ride a bike is by experience.

Experience doesn't mean competence, although to have competence you need experience, not every experience gives you competence. Wikipedia has a very good definition of experience:[49]

Experience is the first-person effects or influence of an event or subject gained through involvement in or exposure to it.

Let's review each of its parts.

Experience is personal

You can't get experience in the shoes of others. What you learn from others is information and a certain kind of knowledge.

You can get *a priori* knowledge — previous to experience —,

---

[49] "Experience." In *Wikipedia*, February 28, 2023. https://en.wikipedia.org/ w/index.php?title=Experience&oldid=1142037327.

theoretical knowledge, or propositional knowledge — the one you memorize or learn with flash-card repetition, from other persons but not the knowledge that comes from experience.

You experience with your senses, perceptions, feelings, thoughts, imagination, and emotions. All your cognitive processes are part of an experience, even the unconscious.

"You had to be there" or "It's a first-hand experience" are the right expressions when talking about an experience.

That's why experience is subjective: everyone experiences things differently.

Experience produces effects

You can read a marketing book or a productivity blog and nothing happens after. You may remember what you read when having a conversation with a colleague or your partner and even share it, but that's it.

Experience changes you, leaves you scars or marks, or at least, it changes your brain.

"It's like riding a bike, you never forget it", it's a very good example of how we intuitively understand knowledge by experience.

Experience influences you

Experience, and what you learn from it, can be unconscious. You learn your mother-tongue language without knowing it, for example.

The effects and influence aren't necessarily always good. Well, in origin, every learning from experience is useful and good. But experience is always lived within a context or circumstance. The context or circumstance can change and the learning becomes obsolete and useless.

That's the case with mental trauma, for example. Fear is useful and good when exposed to dangerous environments. But fear without reason can be an obstacle to life.

You can change your experience with another experience.

Experience is gained

You don't *get* experience. You *gain* experience.

Information goes "in one ear and out of the other" like my grandma used to say about the advice she gave me and I didn't get.

Experience is — in essence — good, desirable, and even profitable. You get or obtain experience and then it's yours and stays with you.

Even when it's not always measurable, experience has some sense of weight, consistency, or physical property.

Sometimes you can't get rid of experiences even if you want. That's where the "beginner's mind" concept applies. Previous experiences can get in the way of new ones.

Experience entails involvement or exposure

You didn't learn that fire burns you by getting exposed to a movie about the fire. You have to go outside of your computer, your office, or your home, but above all, you have to be exposed to experience.

To be exposed means to be "deprived of shelter, protection, or care; subject to risk from a harmful action or condition".

Yes, to experience is to be vulnerable.

The experience of the UX designer

There is a saying, if you want to be a writer, read. If you want to be a musician, listen to music.

Be the user—mindful user—of the object you are designing.

Use the objects your competence is designing.

Learn to fail, learn to fall. Learn from it.

Use your everyday objects as a designer as much as the next human being. But try to pay attention to yourself as a user, to the object, the interactions, and the environment.

Learn to experience the experience of others. If the data or information says the user likes a TV series or videogame you don't know or like, watch it, play it. Try to like it.

If every team in the league has the same playbook, you must have it. But after that, you have to play the game and gain experience. Remember: you have to be there; observe, sense, smell, taste, ear; gain the scars and burns; feel vulnerable. The knowledge you gain from experience is unique, secret, and only for you.

(Published on Feb 5, 2020, in UX Collective)

13

Neumorphism will not kill the skeuomorphism star

Or, as my three-year-old daughter says, "Click here, Granddad!"

Everything began with a couple of stories from Michal Malewicz, here on Medium. Now it's trending in different sites and communities.

Malewicz wrote about a "new skeuomorphism"[50] in UI design. Jason Kelley proposed "neumorphism"[51] for the new trend.

In the beginning, it seemed like a new aesthetic proposal. Original, but only in the design sense. But as the term became viral in specialized sites and communities, it also became a

---

[50] Malewicz, Michal. "What's the next UI Design Trend?" Medium, June 2, 2021. https://uxdesign.cc/whats-the-next-ui-design-trend-75c8b61f5c 7c.

[51] Kelley, Jason. "Neuomorphism?" Medium (blog), December 3, 2019. https://medium.com/@jason_kelley/neuomorphism-2c4cbe84caae.

discussion about neumorphism as a replacement for the flat design trend.

Some of the discussions involve terms like usability, accessibility, adaptability, and even biomorphism.

And of course, skeuomorphism.

Let's start with definitions: neumorphism is a *form, new*, but form. Skeuomorphism is not just a *form*, but a *container*, a vehicle.

> *The term* skeuomorph *is compounded from* skeuos *(σκεῦος), meaning "container or tool", and* morphḗ *(μορφή), meaning "shape"—Wikipedia*[52]

On silent films, intertitles, and interpreters

In the beginning of cinema (silent film era), every projection was accompanied by music played live, and by an interpreter who explained the film to the public.

Yes, a person explained the silent film during the projection.

The theatrical part—the drama—was perfectly understood by the audience. But not the montage, the sequence of shots that build the plot.

The use of intertitle cards and interpreters was necessary to understand the plot for most of the audience.

Intertitle cards and interpreters were the interfaces between the movie and the audience.

Of course, once the audience learned the language of cinema, the intertitles and interpreters were no longer necessary. The

---

[52] "Skeuomorph." In *Wikipedia*, May 17, 2023. https://en.wikipedia.org/w/index.php?title=Skeuomorph&oldid=1155265210.

interface became implicit for the people.

In other words, once the audience understood the *form*, the *container* or the vehicle was no longer necessary.

Well, not for everyone. My daughters (from three to fourteen years old) understand very complicated movies or TV series that are difficult for my parents (from seventy to eighty years old).

When my eldest daughter explains to my mother an element of the plot hidden in a complex montage of a movie—obvious for the young, inconspicuous for the old one—, my daughter becomes an interface.

What is an interface, anyway?

Design is no longer a print to look at or a furnishing to use. Design is now about interactions and experiences.

That doesn't mean that we can forget the communication factor of every design. Therefore, language.

Let's remember a little about Semiotics.

The designer is the sender, the interface is the message, and the user is the receiver. The message is coded, composed of ruled signs, a language.

Every interface is some kind of interpreter between a machine and a human, a software program (now called an app), and a user.

In the current apps, we call a button a button because of previous knowledge of what a button is in the physical world, no matter if it looks like a physical button or not.

You can say a digital button is a metaphor for a physical button. Or you can say it's a metonymy. Anyway, there is a referent and there is a reference.

From an unidentified webcomic, according to The Verge[53]

The interface is a message

When Marshall McLuhan introduced its famous phrase "the medium is the message", it was considered just a way to call for attention. It was difficult to understand that the cinema itself was a message and not just the content of the movies.

Today, it should be clear that an interface is a medium, therefore, an interface is a message.

For me, the save icon on a button in an app is a metaphor or metonymy of a floppy disk. For my daughter, the icon means directly "save". And a floppy disk is a physical representation of the "save" icon.

When a designer mimics an object to design another—called a derivative—retaining ornamental attributes in the new one that is no longer functional, the designer is using skeuomorphism: light bulbs were derivatives from candles, automobiles

---

[53] Farokhmanesh, Megan. "Why Is This Floppy Disk Joke Still Haunting the Internet?" The Verge, October 24, 2017. https://www.theverge.com/2017/10/24/16505912/floppy-disk-3d-print-save-joke-meme.

from horse carts, and radio receivers from phonographs.

The skeuomorphism can be a resource that works as an interpreter, container or vehicle in the use of transitional objects or forms—although it can be a simple design style, of course.

You can experience and learn to use an app using your previous experience and knowledge using physical objects: volume dial, keyboard, switch button...

But once we learn to use the digital object, the skeuomorphism is no longer necessary. Once we get used to the form, we no longer need the container.

The first apps for the iPhone were very skeuomorphic. Then came the material design, with its minimalism and functionalism.

But the material design style was only possible because we, the users, learned to use digital interfaces without the need for physical references.

Well, not for everyone. Do you remember the language of films?

My daughters (especially the youngest) interact seamlessly with the apps and games on their smartphones or tablets. Simpler apps are difficult if not impossible for my parents.

For my three-year-old daughter, a flat design button is a button. For my father, it is a colored rectangle with some text on it.

With a limited verbal vocabulary, my little daughter becomes an interface when she says "Touch here, Granddad!" pointing to a colored square or a picture thumb.

(By the way, my dad's response is "How does she know that?".)

Conclusions

If you are making a movie for my parents, be gentle with the montage and camera movements, please. If you are designing an app for my parents, you have to use skeuomorphism. It's not an aesthetic decision.

But if you are making a movie or designing an app for your daughters, you have more aesthetic freedom. Make complex montages, move the camera, and use material design.

The use of skeuomorphism can be minimalistic or prodigal. There is no need to go baroque with skeuomorphism. In fact, I think that the real problem with skeuomorphism was not the mimic aspect of it, but the non-minimalistic and non-functional approach of its use in digital design.

The skeuomorphism in UI design will die someday in the future, like the need for intertitle cards and interpreters in the movies.

But not yet. There are *personas* in the design of user experiences and interfaces that still need a container, a vehicle, or an interpreter, to understand the form.

My parents still need it.

(Published on Jan 6, 2020, in UX Collective)

14

Two dark experiences with dark mode

More than just readability and battery saving

At night, I read a book to my three-year-old daughter until she sleeps, but I stay some more minutes in the dark, next to her. I have to be sure that she is deeply sleeping before I leave.

If she wakes up just minutes after getting sleep, we have to start over the bed routine.

What would any reasonable person do in these circumstances? Get out of the cell phone and open an app, of course.

This is the problem: if the app doesn't have dark mode implemented and is mostly white or light-colored, it can be like lighting the room with a lamp and my daughter can wake up.

This is not a readability problem. It's a usability problem.

And it's not just for parents like me. The same happens when you are in a dark place like a theater or cinema and you want to be discreet when opening your cell phone.

Background

Steven Hoober has written a very extensive article [54]with 2020 updates to the subject that is a very good starting point for any designer interested (just the notes on contrast are worth it, besides the dark mode topic).

The two main reasons in favor of a dark mode option for an app or website are readability and battery saving.

Apple highlights the readability benefit:

> *Dark Mode puts the focus on the content areas of your interface, allowing that content to stand out while the surrounding UI recedes into the background.* —*Apple Human Interface Guidelines* [55]

Google, besides readability, highlights battery saving.

> *Dark themes reduce the luminance emitted by device screens, while still meeting minimum color contrast ratios. They help improve visual ergonomics by reducing eye strain, adjusting brightness to current lighting conditions, and facilitating screen use in dark environments —all while conserving battery power.* —*Google Material Design* [56]

---

[54] "Dark Isn't Just a Mode:: UXmatters." Accessed May 25, 2023. https://www.uxmatters.com/mt/archives/2020/01/dark-isnt-just-a-mode.php.

[55] Apple Developer Documentation. "Dark Mode." Accessed May 25, 2023. https://developer.apple.com/design/human-interface-guidelines/dark-mode.

[56] Material Design. "Material Design." Accessed May 25, 2023. https://m2.material.io/design/color/dark-theme.html#usage.

For success, the readability depends on the kind of content—text, video, photo, font sizes, etc.—and the way the color palette is implemented—contrast is crucial, as Steven Hoover points out.

A photo gallery, for example, doesn't make much difference because the photos use most of the space on the display and they are not going to change in dark mode.

The success of the battery saving can be very relative if not it's measured properly. It only works with OLED displays[57]. When the original app is mostly white, like most news sites, battery-saving could be significant. Otherwise, like a gray vs true black UI, not so much[58].

The research is poor in this field and the variety of situations versus the very different kinds of apps is overwhelming.

> *Anyway, the few applicable research studies I've found indicate that dark mode is not quite as readable in the dark as one would expect, relative to light mode. Now, this is very narrow research, so didn't account for screens being in outdoor-brightness mode and so on. It also involved a fairly standard test of readability, with text as the content being consumed.—Steven Hoober[59]*

---

[57] Welch, Chris. "Google Confirms Dark Mode Is a Huge Help for Battery Life on Android." The Verge, November 8, 2018. https://www.theverge.com/2018/11/8/18076502/google-dark-mode-android-battery-life.

[58] Ranjbaran, Arash. "What Is Wrong with the Dark Mode?" Medium, October 9, 2019. https://uxdesign.cc/what-is-wrong-with-the-dark-mode-d518 33e01926.

[59] "Dark Isn't Just a Mode:: UXmatters." Accessed May 25, 2023. https://www.uxmatters.com/mt/archives/2020/01/dark-isnt-just-a-mode.php.

There are several articles that have covered this from the design point of view (What is wrong with the dark mode UX?[60], Turn the lights off — designing for dark mode[61], The past, present, and future of Dark Mode[62], just to mention a few).

Here, I just want to talk about two situations on opposite sides of the experience.

Dark mode makes me sleep

As we said above, dark mode is good for better focus attention when reading, according to some.

Maybe, but I have noticed that this focus enhancement lasts just a couple of minutes before I get sleepy.

Low or dim light is good to get sleep. In fact, its use is a recommended practice to overcome insomnia. So, I guess — no research for this — this is the reason that I get sleepy when reading in dark mode.

The absence of light is a cue to my brain to go to sleep.

I can read more on a paper book or a Kindle, for example — using a bed lamp and avoiding the temptation of depending just on de display's backlight in the case of the Kindle.

Here, the light in the room is the cue to my brain to keep it

---

[60] Ranjbaran, Arash. "What Is Wrong with the Dark Mode?" Medium, October 9, 2019. https://uxdesign.cc/what-is-wrong-with-the-dark-mode-d518 33e01926.

[61] Priambodo, Briandito. "Turn the Lights off — Designing for Dark Mode 🌑🌓)." Medium, November 6, 2019. https://uxdesign.cc/turn-the-lights-off-designing-the-dark-mode-of-wego-ios-app-6c4967e59dd6.

[62] Berni, Olivier. "The Past, Present, and Future of Dark Mode." Medium, December 31, 2019. https://uxdesign.cc/the-past-present-and-future-of-dark-mode-9254f2956ec7.

awake.

This is very important because in too many situations you want the user to be awake. Or at least stay alert.

Imagine that you have done an attractive interface that makes the user stay in the app, but as soon the night comes and automatically turns to dark mode, the interface becomes unattractive. That's probably not what you want.

The unbearable lightness of blue light studies

This "sleepy effect" could be contradictory to the famous blue light that comes from the display on computers and smartphones.

The dark mode isn't black. Blue light is the principal light in the spectrum emitted by a modern display. We use to think of black as the absence of color because of our use of indirect light. But in smartphones, tablets, and computers, you evidently can distinguish between a screen turned off and a black interface.

Recently, some inconclusive studies pointed to late-night use of devices as the cause of sleep problems[63] and even retinal cell damage with high-intensity exposure.

But a very recent study, published in December 2019, showed different results that contradicted the previous:

> *Contrary to common belief, blue light may not be as disruptive to our sleep patterns as originally thought — according to scientists. According to the team, using dim,*

---

[63] Miller, Korin. "The Best Blue Light Blocking Glasses To Protect Your Eyes." Forbes. Accessed May 25, 2023. https://www.forbes.com/sites/forbes-personal-shopper/article/best-blue-light-blocking-glasses/.

cooler, lights in the evening and bright warmer lights in the day may be more beneficial to our health. —*Science Daily*[64]

But both studies were done in mice, anyway, and it looks like the human eye is a little different than the mice's.

On the other hand, sunny daylight is 100,000 times brighter than a computer display[65], so it's difficult to think that the display of a cellphone can change our behavior so much.

So, the conclusion is that there is no conclusion yet for dark mode effectiveness, nither for blue light effect[66].

On the opposite sides of the experience

Dark mode requires research yet. Scientific research, yes, but especially, UX research.

Every app or website has particular characteristics, it's used in different situations, and has different kind of users—or indirect users, like my daughter or the people at the theater.

Dark mode can be good for readability but not for engagement. Dark mode can be good for being discreet using an app but not necessarily for battery saving.

---

[64] ScienceDaily. "Blue Light May Not Be as Disruptive to Our Sleep Patterns as Originally Thought." Accessed May 25, 2023. https://www.sciencedaily.com/releases/2019/12/191216173654.htm.

[65] Yuhas, Phillip. "Blue Light Isn't the Main Source of Eye Fatigue and Sleep Loss – It's Your Computer." The Conversation, October 11, 2019. http://theconversation.com/blue-light-isnt-the-main-source-of-eye-fatigue-and-sleep-loss-its-your-computer-124235.

[66] Time. "Forget What You Think You Know About Blue Light and Sleep," January 10, 2020. https://time.com/5752454/blue-light-sleep/.

And don't forget that when doubt exists, leave the user to test and choose. I prefer dark mode when getting my daughter to bed, but I prefer light mode to read and not getting sleep.

(Published on Jan 15, 2020, in UX Collective)

15

New research on digital addiction (and what to think about it)

Because the ethical factor is always important

A recent study following 385 adolescents for six years, found that 72% of them do not play in a way that is harmful or addictive. Another 18% started with moderate symptoms that did not change over time. But 10%, though, showed increased levels of pathological gaming symptoms throughout the study.[67]

The study, led by Sarah M. Coyne of Brigham Young University, was published in May of this 2020 and has brought the digital addiction issue back into the discussion.

Questionnaires applied during six years measured depression, anxiety, aggression, delinquency, empathy, prosocial

---

[67] ScienceDaily. "Is Video Game Addiction Real?" Accessed March 16, 2023. https://www.sciencedaily.com/releases/2020/05/200513143803.htm.

behavior, shyness, sensory reactivity, financial stress, and problematic cell phone use. At the initial point, the results for all these variables were the same in the study group, but after six years 10% displayed higher levels in these variables, especially in depression, aggression, shyness, problematic cell phone use, and anxiety by emerging adulthood.

We can speculate that 10% developed addictive behaviors for causes beyond video games, but we can't assure that those causes are enough to have 10% of addictive adolescents in the group. Without video games, would the rate have been of less than 10%? Would the adolescents have developed another addiction — that may be even more harmful?

We would never know because there is no way to do a six-year study with adolescents away from video games and compare them with another group of gamers.

But what it's important about these kinds of studies is that there is always a percentage of people that, for different circumstances, are going to be susceptible to developing some kind of addictive or unhealthy behaviors while others don't.

Design and behavior

Do you remember that there is also a percentage of *early adopters* and *heavy users* in any content, product, or service, especially in digital form? Have you thought about why?

Early adopters, for instance, are in the range between 13%[68]

---

[68] "Index." Accessed March 16, 2023. https://www.ou.edu/deptcomm/dodjc/groups/99A2/theories.htm.

and 28%[69] according to different studies. Or, following the Pareto principle, 20% of your customers or users represent 80% of your sales or subscription income.[70]

But let's avoid the temptation of useless correlations. What we have to recognize in the data is that even if we consciously try to break the cycle of designing for addictive engagement, some percentage of people are going to fall into it.[71]

In another study, Erik Peper and Richard Harvey from San Francisco State University argued that the overuse of smartphones is just like any other type of substance abuse. Behavioral addiction begins forming neurological connections in the brain in ways similar to how drug addiction is experienced by people — gradually.[72]

"This suggests that these seemingly 'pathological features' of addiction may in fact reflect a normal cognitive process — that we are all to some degree 'wired' to

[69] Kennedy, Brian, and Cary Funk. "28% of Americans Are 'Strong' Early Adopters of Technology." *Pew Research Center* (blog). Accessed March 16, 2023. https://www.pewresearch.org/fact-tank/2016/07/12/28-of-americans-are-strong-early-adopters-of-technology/.

[70] Lavinsky, Dave. "Pareto Principle: How To Use It To Dramatically Grow Your Business." Forbes. Accessed March 16, 2023. https://www.forbes.com/sites/davelavinsky/2014/01/20/pareto-principle-how-to-use-it-to-dramatically-grow-your-business/.

[71] Teixeira, Fabricio. "How Can Designers Help Break the Cycle of Designing for Addiction?" Medium, May 27, 2019. https://uxdesign.cc/how-can-designers-help-break-the-cycle-of-designing-for-addiction-4295f400287f.

[72] ScienceDaily. "We Are All 'wired' for Addiction, Says Researcher." Accessed March 16, 2023. https://www.sciencedaily.com/releases/2016/08/160824172706.htm.

become addicted."

Experience design works with dopamine, motivation, reward system, attention, and learning, in the same way, a school teacher did a century ago trying to make her or his classes more attractive, motivational, and engaging.

The difference between a current experience designer and an old school teacher is that today the former has powerful tools that exponentially increase the effects on the people.

In another analogy, war has always existed but the damage of a bow and arrow doesn't compare to an atomic bomb.

It's not about high technology. Books — the old bounded printed paper pages — can be addictive too. Ask *Harry Potter*'s fans.

We want users, customers, or the audience to be attracted to our content, product, or service. We want them to raise interest in them, to make them feel good or comfortable in their interactions — ergo, to feel pleasure — and to make them come back for more.

In some way, we want them to develop some addiction to our content, product, or service. We play with the idea that strategies like gamification help us to convey our goals without hurting our clients or audience. But we must be aware.

We're not talking about 90% of users or fans. We are talking about 10%. Or a little more or a little less, it doesn't matter. There is going to be a percentage of more susceptible users to addiction.

Beyond design, beyond addiction

Is our content, product, or service as harmless as *Harry Potter*'s book can be? Or is it as harmful as an intensive interactive violent video game can be? Are we engaging our users in a healthy experience or an unhealthy one?

This goes beyond design and technology. It's part of every form of art and communication.

For instance, after a celebrity commits suicide and the media makes extensive coverage, the suicide rate in the population increases.[73]

Unfortunately, a suicide narrative doesn't have to be real. Copycat suicides happen even with fictional narratives.

The publication and success of the novel *The Sorrows of the Young Werther* of Goethe in 1774 brought with it not only the clothing of the character became fashionable in Europe, but also suicide. It's called "the Werther effect".[74]

More recently, the Netflix show *13 Reasons Why,* which narrates a fictional teen's suicide, was associated with the increase in suicides in 10- to 19-year-olds in the United States in the 3 months following its release.[75]

---

[73] "Copycat Suicide." In *Wikipedia*, February 22, 2023. https://en.wikipedia.o rg/w/index.php?title=Copycat_suicide&oldid=1140859527.

[74] "*The Sorrows of Young Werther.*" In *Wikipedia*, January 12, 2023. https://e n.wikipedia.org/w/index.php?title=The_Sorrows_of_Young_Werther& oldid=1133144585.

[75] Niederkrotenthaler, Thomas, Steven Stack, Benedikt Till, Mark Sinyor, Jane Pirkis, David Garcia, Ian R. H. Rockett, and Ulrich S. Tran. "Association of Increased Youth Suicides in the United States With the Release of 13 Reasons Why." *JAMA Psychiatry* 76, no. 9 (September 1, 2019): 933–40. https://doi.org/10.1001/jamapsychiatry.2019.0922.

Let's be clear about some things here.

First, neither Goethe nor Netflix has the intention to provoke "the Werther effect", of course.

Second, this is obviously an extreme example whose goal is to establish awareness about an always-existent minority of users, customers, or audiences, that are more susceptible to an unhealthy engagement with content, product, or service.

And third, the key is in the word "susceptible". Addiction or unhealthy behavior is not caused by the content, product, or service—it only has an effect on those who are susceptible.

An "educational" app

Let's mention an example that is not at the extreme of the spectrum.

Recently, a company tried to sell an educational app service to my daughter's school. A typical app that uses gamification to engage the students to do some lessons and exercises progressively and incrementally. Ideal for distance learning. Some of the parents agreed to let their children be testers of the app, and they reported that their kids liked it a lot. "They couldn't stop using it", were their words. The kids were advancing to different levels of the app very fast, almost finishing all the lessons that they received.

Let's pause a little.

Can you see the potential damage? "They couldn't stop using it". The fact that it is an "educational app" doesn't make it good behavior. This kind of app can be good for approximately 90% of young students that are not susceptible to addictive behaviors. But, what about the other 10% or so?

Other educational app services don't let the students use the service or the app for more than a couple of levels or they are time-limited. The reasons are to avoid compulsive or addictive behaviors as much as to promote spaced repetition for effective learning, and evidence-based techniques.[76]

A kid—and any person—can't use an app all day, no matter how "educational" can be.

Ethics and the susceptible minority

We can't stop ourselves from writing the next *Werther* or *Catcher in the Rye,* because the effects were unintentional and unpredictable. But we could stop for realizing the second season of a series like *13 Reasons Why,* after what the data showed.

In the case of products and services, there are important guides and discussions on the topic.[77] Let's add some points to the reflection.

1. There are no answers, rules, or principles here. Morality is about rules, principles, and even laws that answer the question of how to behave.
2. Ethics belongs to Philosophy and is a discipline in constant questioning of behaviors and how we should act.

---

[76] Smolen, Paul, Yili Zhang, and John H. Byrne. "The Right Time to Learn: Mechanisms and Optimization of Spaced Learning." *Nature Reviews. Neuroscience* 17, no. 2 (February 2016): 77–88. https://doi.org/10.1038/nrn.2015.18.

[77] Teixeira, Fabricio. "How Can Designers Help Break the Cycle of Designing for Addiction?" Medium, May 27, 2019. https://uxdesign.cc/how-can-designers-help-break-the-cycle-of-designing-for-addiction-4295f400287f.

For Ethics, there are no absolute answers but continuous observation, reflection, and discussion. In the extreme examples I used above, there are ethical solutions. The World Health Organization has published a guide for media professionals about how to handle suicide cases to prevent unwanted effects.[78] Some countries, like Norway, have journalism codes to avoid mentions of the subject.

3. We have to pay attention to the experience we design in terms of how addictive or unhealthy it can be. We have to reflect on it and keep the discussion going. Remember, there are no rules, and even if you get some answers in the form of rules, they are going to be obsolete or have to be updated.

4. And to counteract the "Werther effect" there is the "Papageno effect"—the protective effects of positive stories, refusing to publicize suicide events, or changing the way that they are depicted. Counteract possible unintentional and unpredictable negative effects with intentional and predictable positive effects.[79]

5. We have to consult experts in the field of our content, product, or service. If we are designing and developing an educational app, we have to be near educational experts—psychologists, pedagogues, teachers, parents... Or if our users are going to be older adults, we need

---

[78] "Preventing Suicide: A Resource for Media Professionals (Update 2017)." Accessed March 16, 2023. https://apps.who.int/iris/bitstream/handle/106 65/258814/WHO-MSD-MER-17.5-eng.pdf.

[79] Sisask, Merike, and Airi Värnik. "Media Roles in Suicide Prevention: A Systematic Review." *International Journal of Environmental Research and Public Health* 9, no. 1 (January 2012): 123–38. https://doi.org/10.3390/ ijerph9010123.

    gerontologists in our team.

6. But for any target or user, customer or audience, we have to be aware of the "susceptible minority".

In this area, we can't say that content, product, or service is good for the majority of the users, customers, or audience. We have to turn our attention to that 10% or what-ever-percentage that is susceptible to addictive or unhealthy behaviors.

(Published on Jul 9, 2020, in UX Collective)

III

On UX Writing and other skills

16

What if UX writing was more like screenwriting than copywriting?

Crossing disciplines to find knowledge

User experience design is a term born from human-computer interaction design but it extends now to a wider conception of *product*—and even service.

In the film and TV industry, the product is a movie or a TV show, or a series. They are products that produce experiences. The people producing them are not just very good at giving experiences to an audience—they have a lot of experience doing it.

Unlike the IT industry, a production team is led by the writing, not by the design. This writing is technical, with a lot of observations, calls, and instructions, besides the dialogs: it's called screenwriting.

The screenplay is the base and origin of the whole process. The director of a movie or the producer of a TV program has a photographic sense — some of them are very good photographers — but the construction of the visual media is based on writing.

Even the storyboard — when used — is elaborated on in the screenplay.

There are exceptions, of course. The director or producer could work just with an outline or a general idea. That's mainly the case in documentaries, sports, or reality shows. The outline works as a container of events to record.

A little Archaeology

The creation of the user experience field emerged, first, from the engineering of human-computer interaction, and then, from the software development process.

Later, when usability and aesthetics began to be a concern in the elaboration of new technology devices, the design was incorporated into the process. In the last stage of the process, by the way.

At that time, the production of technological devices was led by computer engineers first, software developers, later, and just in the last decades, by designers, particularly visual designers.

The stages in the production process inherited the chronological sequence: the form followed the function. A computer was a black box that the designer had to make look nice.

As the technical factors of production became less relevant, the developers and designers started to lead the way.

Now designers start with wireframes and prototypes and developers and engineers resolve after them.

It is no accident that Donald Norman, a psychologist with

an engineering background, had brought the user experience concept to the new field. He covered all the knowledge needed, from the most abstract and technical to the most practical and subjective. A little engineering, developing, and design, under the shelter of psychology.

Once the scale moved towards the psychological aspects of the experience, the best prepared to talk about perceptions, emotions, attitudes, or affections in a team composed of engineers, developers, and designers, were the latter.

We call it UX design and not UX engineering or UX developing.

The arrival of UX writing

The production team expanded and became more interdisciplinary, including marketing, management, distribution, packaging...

In this integration and interdisciplinary, one of the things that became important in the user experience of the product was the texts.

"Unexpected catastrophic failure" as an error message didn't look good on a dialog box neither gave a good user experience.

Evidently, there were no writers in the team—not to say specialized writers given the novelty of the tasks needed to accomplish. A writer thinks about the readers. Writers came from marketing. Yes, some were designers or engineers that were good at writing, but most of them came from a more writing-based background.

> ... finally, organizations are realizing that copywriting shouldn't only land on the marketing team's

desk.—Kristina Bjoran[80]

Today, mainly because the designers are leading the teams, the design of the user experience is very visual—prototypes, wireframes, and user flow.

Exceptions apply here too. In UX design we can start with user stories, briefings, or requirements. But most of the time, they are used more as inspiration, reference, and a constant reminder of the final goal.

A UX writer, then, produces the text elements to be used by the UX designer. The texts are seen as graphic elements even when they are texts. First is the visual composition, then the texts.[81]

> *All too often product developers think of UI text as something that belongs to product documentation phase. "First we'll design the product, and then we'll hire someone to help us write a UI copy." Such assumptions often cause a lot of harm because critical UI issue can go unnoticed until the later stages of product development process.— Nick Babich*[82]

The UX designer doesn't use UX writing, uses texts (copy, labels, instructions, commands...).

---

[80] "What Is UX Writing? | UX Booth." Accessed April 24, 2023. https://www.uxbooth.com/articles/what-is-ux-writing/.

[81] Pope, Lauren. "Art and Copy: Bridging the Gap between Design and Content." Medium, March 23, 2020. https://uxdesign.cc/art-and-copy-bridging-the-gap-between-design-and-content-4325b0939134.

[82] Babich, Nick. "16 Rules of Effective UX Writing." Medium, April 8, 2022. https://uxplanet.org/16-rules-of-effective-ux-writing-2a20cf85fdbf.

The text, known to digital designers as Lorem Ipsum or "filler text", is essentially a temporary placeholder for the text. It's commonly used in the graphic, print and publishing industries for previewing visual mockups before the final copy is entered. —iFactory[83]

UX writing is what this specialized writer does, not what she or he produces. A UX writer produces text.

In this sense, UX writing is very similar to copywriting. Not because of their goals and work areas — they are very different — but because the outcome or product of both writings is texts to be used as elements within the product or service.

What if...

When I read "UX writing", two different meanings come to my mind.

First, the actual meaning is the act of writing the text for the user experience.

But next, I think in the act of writing the user experience. To describe, step by step, scene by scene, the experience itself.

What if UX writing was more screenwriting than copywriting?

I have imagined a user experience design based on a screenplay. A little absurd, but illuminating, like any thought experiment.

What if the UX design was led by writers — like in the movie

---

[83] iFactory. "How Lorem Ipsum Became Web Design Standard." *Medium* (blog), January 10, 2018. https://medium.com/@iFactoryDigital/how-lorem-ipsum-became-web-design-standard-6260377682f4.

business—and not by designers?

> *Here's where I'd like to draw the parallel with writ-*
> *ing—because a core skill of the interaction designer is*
> *imagining users (characters), motivations, actions, reac-*
> *tions, obstacles, successes, and a complete set of "what*
> *if" scenarios. These are the skills of a writer—Susan*
> *Stuart*[84]

"We need the visuals!", the team could say. But there is nothing more visual than movies, and the film direction and production are based on screenplays, not visuals.

You don't pitch a film to Hollywood investors with prototypes or wireframes. You pitch a film with a screenplay.

Yes, I know film and apps are different products. But remember, this is a thought experiment crossing disciplines to find knowledge.

When the production was led by the engineers, there was more written documentation. Not because they liked to write, but because it was indispensable.

For software development, engineers used to work with a Software Design Document.[85] A very technical document including terms like data design (with objects and structures), architecture, interface, and procedural design. There is an IEEE standard for it.

---

[84] Stuart, Susan. "Why UX Design Is a Lot Like Writing (Not Just Art-Making)." Medium, April 26, 2016. https://blog.prototypr.io/why-creating-a-ux-is-like-writing-often-more-than-art-288efae9523e.

[85] "Software Design Description." In *Wikipedia*, August 22, 2022. https://en .wikipedia.org/w/index.php?title=Software_design_description&oldid=1 105986397.

That standard document or similar is still required when working for government agencies for legal purposes, mainly. Nobody writes it unless it is asked but engineers don't usually read it anymore.

Engineers now work with roadmaps and Kanban boards (visuals!), from very general descriptions of the big project to detailed requirements for specific functions or necessities.

However, these are very technical documents only used by the developers, not the whole team.

A detour through the Agile methodologies

The most efficient and effective method of conveying information to and within a development team is face-to-face conversation. —*The Agile Manifesto*[86]

There is an old debate between the proponents of the Agile methodologies and 'old school' developers about how much-written documentation a project should have.

The Agile Manifesto was originally about development, not design. But its philosophy has permeated project management, product management, and of course, UX design.

Agile software development values "working software over comprehensive documentation" and "responding to change over following a plan", among others.[87] But there is no detailed explanation or reason why the former is better than the latter.

---

[86] "Principles behind the Agile Manifesto." Accessed April 24, 2023. http://ag ilemanifesto.org/principles.html.

[87] "Manifesto for Agile Software Development." Accessed April 24, 2023. http://agilemanifesto.org/.

It is no accident that the base document for the Agile methodologies is a manifesto, with just a few words, and very ambiguous concepts. This is very coherent with its own philosophy, but it also refutes the necessity of a well-written document.

You can produce good products on time and have good documentation and a detailed plan. Ask the film industry.

(I'm not against Agile methodologies. I've worked with them and like any methodology, there are projects that are ideal for it.)

Why not?

A better example of a possible UX design driven by writing is the Game Design Document used in game development.[88] Not a standard, but as video games are becoming more complex and more a movie-like experience, this document has become the screenplay of the industry.

> *Characters, actions, scenarios and enough visual sensibility to bring those things to life in a (primarily) visual medium — that's what's needed in a screenwriter/ director, and also in creating the foundation of a good application design. —Susan Stuart*[89]

I have some hypotheses of why UX design is driven by visuals

---

[88] "Game Design Document." In *Wikipedia*, February 6, 2023. https://en.wiki pedia.org/w/index.php?title=Game_design_document&oldid=113784271 8.

[89] Stuart, Susan. "Why UX Design Is a Lot Like Writing (Not Just Art-Making)." Medium, April 26, 2016. https://blog.prototypr.io/why-creating-a-ux-is-like-writing-often-more-than-art-288efae9523e.

more than writing. The same applies to why Agile methodologies, in general, are a trend in the industry.

We don't have enough time to read. Or we don't want to read. Sometimes, we can't read.

We don't have enough time to write. Or we don't want to write. Sometimes, we can't write.

New generations prefer visuals over text. Not just the users but the designers, developers, marketers... One of the reasons too why we prefer meetings with PowerPoints and not emails with documentation to discuss.

(The readers of Medium may disagree with these hypotheses. But Medium readers are biased: they are here because they like to read and/or write. If not, they were on Youtube.)

Language is another problem. English is the *lingua franca* for the industry, but this is not enough yet to let us work with remote teams and different mother-tongue languages among them.

Crossing disciplines to find knowledge

We have to learn from other ways to design user experiences. Not just to design better user experiences but to improve the methods to do it. The film industry is just an example.

We have to be careful with doing the things we do just because "that's the way we always have done it".

We have to check if the reasons to use the resources and tools we have are because of a lack of skills or knowledge and not because they are the best options.

We don't have to take full methods or processes from one discipline to the other, but we can learn specific ways and techniques from them.

121

(Published on Jan 9, 2020 in UX Collective)

17

All writing is UX writing

Lessons from a tell-tale heart and learning to write music

I remember the first time I experienced reading a story.

I mean, not the first time I *read* a story, but the first time I *experienced* a story.

It was The Tell-Tale Heart by Edgar Allan Poe. I was eight years old, I think.

You know the plot.[90] The narrator insists on his mental sanity while listening to the beating heart of the man he killed hidden under the floor. His feelings of guilt and the increasing sound make him confess his crime.

I don't have to say it's a masterpiece. The words and style that the narrator uses in the beginning, are simple, paused, clear and formal, like the sanity he insists on showing.

---

[90] "The Tell-Tale Heart." In *Wikipedia*, March 22, 2023. https://en.wikipedia.org/w/index.php?title=The_Tell-Tale_Heart&oldid=1145995111.

But his language changes gradually until insanity. He starts explaining ideas, but he finishes describing perceptions and sensations. You can hear his screams at the end.

The increasing beating of the heart he listens to is the rhythm of the tale.

I remember the increase of my own heart beating along with my stress, my desperation facing the imminent ending, and above all, the increase of speed in my reading as I went through the words.

Just words.

No interactions, no apps, no clicks, no buttons, no swipes... Just words.

Writing is writing. Marketing writing is writing. Copywriting is writing. And yes, UX writing is writing.

And vice versa: good writing makes good marketing writing, good copywriting, and good UX writing.

Charles Dickens did very good marketing for his serial novels because of his mastery of literary cliffhangers.[91]

A good copy is like the title of a novel. Who can resist picking up a book in a bookshop titled The Lion, the Witch, and the Wardrobe or And Then There Were None?

I'm sure that Edgar Allan Poe would be an excellent UX writer. The text below is from his essay The Philosophy of Composition[92] and it has the tone of a modern manual of UX writing:

Within this limit, the extent of a poem may be made to bear

---

[91] "Cliffhanger." In *Wikipedia*, March 24, 2023. https://en.wikipedia.org/w/index.php?title=Cliffhanger&oldid=1146385729.

[92] "Edgar Allan Poe Society of Baltimore - Works - Tales - The Philosophy of Composition (Text-02)." Accessed May 10, 2023. https://www.eapoe.org/works/essays/philcomp.htm.

mathematical relation to its merit — in other words, to the excitement or elevation — again in other words, to the degree of the true poetical effect which it is capable of inducing; for it is clear that the brevity must be in the direct ratio of the intensity of the intended effect: — this, with one proviso — that a certain degree of duration is absolutely requisite for the production of any effect at all.

In fact, you can check his evolution in writing[93] along with his practice and knowledge of the publishing industry of his time. He learned what the audience liked and wrote more and better for them

We live in the middle of two extremes: hyper-specialization vs over-generalization.

UX writing could be seen as one of the most recent specialization skills of the already specialized UX design.

But on the other extreme is writing. Plain and simple writing.

To be a good UX writer you need to be a good writer. A good writer thinks in his or her audience, tests words and structure, traces a reader or user flow, changes tone and style...

Good writing designs an experience for the reader. All good writing is UX writing.

Any characteristic you can give of a good UX writer, you can find in a good writer.

Words are elements of design. They respond to the rules of composition. You can use long sentences as you use long lines. Words and sentences have color and texture, form and space...

And I'm not talking about typography.

You can set the rhythm of your writing just with words and

---

[93] "Edgar Allan Poe." In *Wikipedia*, May 2, 2023. https://en.wikipedia.org/w/index.php?title=Edgar_Allan_Poe&oldid=1152872188.

sentences. You can make music with them.

> *This sentence has five words. Here are five more words. Five-word sentences are fine. But several together become monotonous. Listen to what is happening. The writing is getting boring. The sound of it drones. It's like a stuck record. The ear demands some variety. Now listen. I vary the sentence length, and I create music. Music. The writing sings. It has a pleasant rhythm, a lilt, a harmony. I use short sentences. And I use sentences of medium length. And sometimes when I am certain the reader is rested, I will engage him with a sentence of considerable length, a sentence that burns with energy and builds with all the impetus of a crescendo, the roll of the drums, the crash of the cymbals–sounds that say listen to this, it is important.*
>
> *So write with a combination of short, medium, and long sentences. Create a sound that pleases the reader's ear. Don't just write words. Write music. —Gary Provost*[94]

This quote is highly known among writers. It should be the first example of good UX writing before seeing titles, labels, cards, buttons, visual flows, interactions, interfaces...

UX writing is writing. All writing is UX writing.

---

[94] "Introduction to Sentence Structure | College Writing Handbook." Accessed May 10, 2023. https://courses.lumenlearning.com/suny-jeffersoncc-styleguide/chapter/introduction-to-sentence-structure/.

(Published on Dec 15, 2019, in UX Collective)

18

Writing design in a French style

Because semioticians know better

"One does not think words, one thinks only phrases." — Paul Valéry

The unit

As the French semioticians knew, the smallest linguistic unit is the phrase, not the word.

Words alone are representations, but they don't have meaning per se. Meaning requires syntax and context. Everybody knows what the word "house" represents. But there is no meaning in "house". Words are just elements and a language is a composition of elements. Only in a phrase, you'll find both, elements and their composition.

Phrases can be as small as one word. "Hello!", is a phrase if it's in the right context. Phrases are smaller than sentences[95]. "Hello! I have been waiting for you since 8 in the morning", is a sentence.

Remember, context is everything in any language.

Let me give you another context. Imagine a traveler that, after a big adventure, comes back home. S/he opens the door and says "Home!". There, the word "home" is more than a representation, it has meaning. It's a phrase.

We write by phrases because writing is about meanings not about representations. Even when we do a simple list as a reminder, we do a list of phrases, not just words. "Coffee, cleaning, Tom, keys", are phrases. Only you know if "Tom" means "call him", "meet him", or "email him".

Another context. You have a contact form on a given website or app. You follow the text fields and buttons, and at the end, on a button or similar, you find the word "Submit". "Submit" has meaning only in the context of the contact form.

In fact, all the words in the contact form work like a phrase. They are not loose words.

---

95 Ediket. "What's the Difference between a Phrase and a Sentence? And What about Clauses? (Part 1)." *Medium* (blog), June 21, 2017. https://m edium.com/@Ediket/what-s-the-difference-between-a-phrase-and-a-sentence-and-what-about-clauses-part-1-c7ae15564e3c.

"Contact", "Name", "Email", and "Send", in the right visual context form a phrase.

After a phrase, you can start a dialog. After you push or click "Send", the answer is "Thank you".

We can do a much better contact form, but let's see some important distinctions first.

Phrases vs sentences

Unfortunately, the English translators use the word "sentence" instead of "phrase", when translating from French.

So, when you read Roland Barthes, you must consider that he is referring to phrases in quotes like this:

> As everyone knows, linguistics stops at the phrase; it is the last unit that falls within its scope; for if the phrase—being an order and not a sequence—is not reducible to the sum of its words, and constitutes therefore an original unit, an enunciation, on the other hand, is nothing but the succession of the phrases it contains. From the point of view of linguistics, there is nothing in discourse that is not matched in the phrase. "The phrase," writes Martinet, "is the smallest segment that is perfectly and systematically representative of discourse."
> — Roland Barthes, An Introduction to the Structural Analysis of Narrative

In this and the other quotes from the French in this article, I have substituted "sentence" by "phrase", to be more accurate with the originals.

This is important because we use to think that writing is

based on words, that our raw material is words:

> *Words are the model, words are the tools, words are the*
> *boards, words are the nails.* —*Richard Rhodes*

But when I read Roland Barthes and the distinction and different levels of function for words, phrases, sentences, paragraphs, etc., in the language, it made more sense how we think
and write.

> *A writer is not someone who expresses his thoughts,*
> *his passion, or his imagination in phrases, but **some-***
> ***one who thinks phrases**: A Phrase-Thinker* —*Roland*
> *Barthes, **The Pleasure of the Text***

"Unicorn" is a beautiful word—at least according to my little
daughter—but our mind always tries to fill empty context and
syntax: "Where did it come from? Is it real?, Why is it here?
Why a unicorn? Am I dreaming?".

Sorry, I'm a skeptic about unicorns, but my daughter may
think of a series of other phrases: "Into the Woods, at the
twilight, blue, magic..."

Texting and designing

This goes beyond narration, dialog, or contact forms. This
is a fundamental distinction to understand when writing, no
matter what kind of writing.

> *Writing is writing. Marketing writing is writing. Copy-*
> *writing is writing. And yes, UX writing is writing.* — *All*

writing is UX writing[96]

The process of writing is done in two phases or steps: one is texting, and the other is designing.

I could say that writing is made by simple writing and designing, but I prefer to use the word "texting" to make a distinction from writing as a whole. The word "texting" is heavily associated with typing messages on the cellphone, but that can be an advantage as we'll see later.

When you write an essay, article, or letter, you can start with an outline. An outline is a design made of phrases. Every element in the outline has a meaning in the context of the outline.

Then, you start writing phrases, sentences, and paragraphs. You may see the relation between them when writing. But in some moments you just write text without thinking about the general structure. For distinction proposes, let's call this phase of pure writing, texting.

When you write a letter, you may write the greeting ("Hello"), an introduction ("The reason for this letter is..."), the main body, etc., not necessarily in an orderly or structured manner.

The products of your texting phase are the greetings, introductions, ideas, stories, descriptions, instructions, points of view...

Here is where the word "texting" shows its value. Texting is done in chunks, and is informal, without much thinking or editing. I'm not using it in a disrespectful manner. On the contrary, no matter if you are writing a little message to a friend

---

[96] Corona, Adolfo Ramírez. "All Writing Is UX Writing." Medium, December 15, 2019. https://uxdesign.cc/all-writing-is-ux-writing-ed0645fbd502.

or writing a philosophical insight, this writing works with the text and just with the text, not with the writing as a whole.

When writing the greeting, for example, you just think of a good way to say hello, not in the letter as a whole.

The other phase is what we usually call editing or composition. Let's call it the designing phase.

When designing you look for an ideal order of the sentences and paragraphs. Some groups of them can be sections, chapters... Here is what you think in the letter as a whole.

It is the moment you ask yourself, "Does the introduction too long?". "Do I have to explain first the previous problem we have?". "Do I have to use another greeting?".

When writing, there are iterations between texting and designing. Designing imposes a change in the text, and a change in the text imposes a change in design.

Sometimes the distinction between both phases is clear. For example, to write an essay the recommendation is to have a session of freewriting, which is mere writing without editing—what I call texting. Freewriting is done without our "inner critic". After that, you edit the piece with that "inner critic". That's what I call designing.

In other cases, the division between phases is imperceptible. You do texting and designing almost at the same time. When you write an informal email, for example, you use text and design almost simultaneously.

When writing a long piece like the one you are reading now, I usually don't have the whole piece clear in my head. I start by texting my thoughts or using previous notes—or better, phrases. Then, the iteration of the design starts.

Other pieces have a specific goal—a particular presentation or an editor requirement—, and I start by designing more than texting. I outline, mind map, make lists, a table of content, questions, bullets... After that, I text the little parts and the iteration begins.

Phases and levels

Writing as a process is done in these two phases. But if we see writing as an object, we see texting and designing as two different levels of it.

Here, the use of the words "texting" and "designing" helps us to understand better how writing works or functions in the design of an interface, product, content, or experience.

UX writing—as any writing—has to contemplate both levels. The text has to have good spelling and grammar, a vocabulary according to the audience, good style, etc. And the design—the composition of the text elements—has to have a logical order, good flow, solid structure, etc.

A contact form can have good text but bad design or vice versa. Let's see first the text and then the design.

```
Text for a contact form:
-----------------------
- Contact us
- Your name
- Your email
- Message or comments
- Send
```

We start with that text, but then we do the composition, the design.

```
Text for a contact form:
------------------------
To contact us, please tell us...
your name,
your email,
what do you need,
send it, and we will contact you.
```

After the first design, we can have an iteration of the text.

Remember

1. The raw material of writing is phrases, not words.
2. Writers think and work with phrases. Think phrases, write phrases.
3. Writing has two phases or steps: texting and designing.
4. Writing is the iteration of texting and designing.
5. This applies no matter if you are writing an interface or a novel.
6. "Unicorn" is a beautiful word.

(Published on Jun 27, 2020, in UX Collective)

19

Is this story real?

The fiction and nonfiction factor in audiences, users, and loved ones

"This reminds me of one of my two daughters", said Jorge Matte, the principal market researcher of the study we were doing. "When I'm going to tell her a bedtime story she always asks 'Is this story real?' If I answer **yes**, she gets ready to listen to it. If **not**, she is uninterested. In some way, she only likes stories that are real."

An insight into research is not an answer to your business questions but rather a revelation about human behavior.

The story of Jorge Matte's daughter was an insight. In the market, audience, or user research, this is one of the milestones you look for intensively. You find only some in your career. I mean, you find many results and answers to your research questions, but insights come once in a while.

An insight needs an explanation because is like an inside joke.

If you don't have the context it's difficult to understand it. But like a eureka moment, once you get it, everything looks clear.

In this case, we were having an informal meeting after the last focus group of several that we had done the weeks before. We were tired but it was important to have some talk about what had happened when our ideas and observations were still fresh.

The study was about the new broadcasting television channel I was working for in Mexico City. It was mainly a news and current affairs channel. Our content was not for massive audiences. We didn't have a budget to buy and program expensive movies or series.

We were looking for a specific audience, for a niche.

That day, I found more than that.

The year was 2004. To start a broadcasting company in Mexico was difficult because there were bigger television channels with a lot of people watching them already, with a lot of Mexican soup operas or *telenovelas*, sitcoms, celebrity gossip shows, corn pop movies, TV series, cartoons, and so on.

They had the usual news programs at specific times: one in the morning, another at midday, and the main news program in the evening.

Our channel had, besides several news programs, political and current affairs talk shows, business and cultural leaders' interviews, and a very good backup of documentaries, mainly from BBC and Discovery Channel.

We wanted to know who was watching us and what do they like to watch, in order to design TV programming and marketing strategies, attract more audience and grow.

As usually happens when you start to market new products, we know what our audience didn't want or like. We knew that there was an audience that didn't want to watch *telenovelas*, sitcoms, celebrity gossip, etc. And we already had some news programs and shows that had some audience, but that wasn't enough if we wanted to design and build a whole product or a brand around a TV channel.

I must confess I was a little skeptical about the focus groups. I am more of a quantitative research guy. But what we found that day are some of the things you can't find in quantitative data.

In qualitative research, the language is very important. Particularly the words. You try to collect the words that the respondents say, group them, make some sets or clusters, and try to find patterns.

The words that the people in those focus groups said when they were asked what they liked about the TV channel and what else they would like to see, were something like these:

I like/want... current affairs, real stories, important issues, reality, the truth, actual persons, relevant news, documentaries, reportages, information... contact, or connection to reality.

On the opposite extreme, these were the words expressed by the people that didn't like our channel:

I like/want... stories, fantasy, nice and beautiful characters or persons, comedy, funny stuff, things to marvel at, fictional stories... disconnect from reality.

Do you see the pattern?

After Jorge Matte told the story of one of her daughters it was clear to us that some people want to consume content that is based on reality.

And, on the other hand, some people want to consume content that is mainly fiction. They want to escape from reality.

"I see, it's like the division in every American book store",

I replied to Jorge and his bedtime story. "There are fiction and nonfiction books. That's the foundation of the American publishing industry!"

Some literary genres overlap between fiction and nonfiction books, like historical, biographical, travel, crime, etc. But the question every reader wants to know the answer to before he buys a book is "Is this story real?".

"So now it's clear. We are a nonfiction TV channel!", I said. "So, even if we program movies or TV series, we have to look for movies or TV series that are based on true stories!".

I should say that the division between fiction and nonfiction books is almost exclusively from North America[97]. It may be a market-based division, I don't know—I haven't found the origin of this classification—but it doesn't exist in other countries. It wasn't obvious to us.

As I said, an insight is like a eureka moment. Since that day sharing insight with Jorge Matte, I see two kinds of audiences—like book readers—for any kind of content depending on this fiction-nonfiction factor.

Even more, I can identify two kinds of personalities depending on the interest or attraction a person has to fiction or nonfiction discourses.

This has helped me a lot in my work, in my psychotherapy and coaching practice, and even more, in my personal life.

I'm a nonfiction person. But my eldest daughter is a fiction person. I prefer to read essays, and articles, and watch dramas or documentaries. My eldest daughter loves fantasy and terror

[97] Lea, Richard. "Fiction v Nonfiction – English Literature's Made-up Divide." *The Guardian*, March 24, 2016, sec. Books. https://www.theguardian.com/books/2016/mar/24/fiction-nonfiction-english-literature-culture-writers-other-languages-stories.

in any form. I love David Fincher's movies. She loves J. K. Rowling's books.

But what is interesting it's that we share our love for science fiction. And also The Lord of the Rings or Titanic. Why? Because they have the right mix for both fiction and nonfiction audiences. Or the right layers. Let me explain.

In science fiction, for example, you have the right mix. You have a fictional story built on known facts. The fictional story usually explores the boundaries of the facts.

> *A handy short definition of almost all science fiction might read: realistic speculation about possible future events, based solidly on adequate knowledge of the real world, past and present, and on a thorough under-standing of the nature and significance of the scientific method. —Robert A. Heinlein[98]*

On the other hand, in The Lord of the Rings, you have a lot of fiction in the main arch and some secondary stories. But the struggle of Frodo against the power of the One Ring is an actual struggle of any human being against any power.

Not to mention how actual the language and historical structure of the novel feels because of the influence that J. R. R. Tolkien had from his philology background[99].

---

[98] "Definitions of Science Fiction." In *Wikipedia*, March 9, 2023. https://en.wikipedia.org/w/index.php?title=Definitions_of_science_fiction&oldid=1143659208.

[99] "J. R. R. Tolkien's Influences." In *Wikipedia*, May 13, 2023. https://en.wikipedia.org/w/index.php?title=J._R._R._Tolkien%27s_influences&oldid=1154641069.

A lot of it is just straight teenage stuff. I didn't mean it to be, but it's perfect for them. I think they're attracted by things that give verisimilitude. —J. R. R. Tolkien[100]

James Cameron's Titanic is a good example. Rose and Jack's story is pure fiction built on the true shipwreck story.

For the movie Titanic, we unearthed every known photograph, poured over architectural drawings and built our ship rivet by rivet, making sure everything was in its rightful place. —James Cameron[101]

So, good content has different layers for different audiences.

Do you want a very different kind of content example?

There are habit-tracking apps. Two examples: *Strides* and *Habitica*. Guess which is for fiction and which is for nonfiction audiences.

---

[100] Plimmer, Charlotte and Denis. "JRR Tolkien: 'Film My Books? It's Easier to Film The Odyssey.'" *The Telegraph*, April 25, 2016. https://www.telegraph .co.uk/films/2016/04/19/jrr-tolkien-film-my-books-its-easier-to-film-the-odyssey/.

[101] USA TODAY. "James Cameron Analyzes What He Got Right and Wrong in 'Titanic: 20 Years Later.'" Accessed May 25, 2023. https://www.usatoday. com/story/life/entertainthis/2017/11/27/james-cameron-titanic/889969 001/.

Strides and Habitica apps screenshots

When I teach, coach or give psychotherapy, I always consider this insight.

I have to give facts, data, and information, all wrapped up in stories but never forget to encourage imagination and fantasy.

For some, I quote scientific research and it is enough for them. For others, I use movies or novel characters as examples.

In meditation or mindfulness, some prefer the breath reference, the mantra without meaning, or the zen-like style. Others prefer visualizations, analogies, or metaphors.

The time has passed since that talk with Jorge Matte. Today I am the one who tells bedtime stories to my daughters. For the eldest one, it is clear that the stories don't have to be real. For the youngest is difficult to say because she is three years old.

However, her preference for toys that simulate work tools, motors, and machines could be a hint of what I'm going to hear in the future.

"Is this story real, Dad?"

(Published on Nov 24, 2019, in UX Collective)

20

A horrid UI in the best OS of all time

A little chronicle of the origin of a revolutionary idea called UX

In 1981, before the development of what we call today user experience design or usability — not to mention the graphic user interface — a Psychology professor from the University of California, San Diego with a little background in electrical engineering, **wrote an article for a computer magazine with a caustic critique of the user interface of the most popular and devoted operating system at the moment**. Its title was 'The Trouble with Unix'.

The group that built Unix didn't take the criticism well. Michael Lesk, a computer scientist who thirteen years later received the *Flame* award for his contributions to Unix, was in charge of responding to the affront.

To start, Michael Lesk argued that **the author of the article didn't have the academic credentials to be taken seriously**. He had seven books published at the time, but all about Psychology.

It didn't help that the professor used an ironic tone at some moments and a ruthless tone at others. Also, he was accused of not having research to support his remarks — even when the developers didn't do any research to design the Unix interface or the magazine was not an academic one — and, worst of all, for not offering a better alternative to the operating system.

Despite the response from the developers, the users who read the article published in *Datamation* loved it. They truly identify with all the problems and the common sense failures or the user interface that the author related. Interestingly enough was the new discipline he was talking about, "so new that it doesn't exist, but it ought to": cognitive engineering. And **the system design principles that he proposed were thought-provoking**: be consistent, provide the user with an explicit model, give feedback, provide sensible memory aids...

In 1988, seven years after the publication of 'The Trouble with Unix' in *Datamation* magazine, **the author published a book that would change design forever**, elevating it to a very deep and complex process and highlighting the attention of the user and the experience: *The Psychology of Everyday Things* (re-edited and published later as *The Design of Everyday Things*).

Yes, the author of that article criticizing the Unix user interface was Don A. Norman, considered today as the founder of UX and the father of cognitive engineering.

What is Unix?

To weigh the importance of the criticism of Unix and its influence on what we call today UX design, we have to know a little about how the operating system worked.

Unix is considered one of the best operating systems of all

time. To give you an idea, Unix is the father of modern Linux and, in some way, macOS is the cousin of Linux itself. New versions of Unix are still in use on some big servers supporting the Internet itself.

Unix was an operating system with a text-based user interface, which means that the user only had access to the system by typing on the keyboard text commands. Experts call it a command-line interface (CLI). Today we deal with graphic user interfaces (GUI) in most of our computers and gadgets, and recently with voice user interfaces (VUI).

The "shell" is like an app that translates text commands to the operating system. To access the shell on your computer today, you'll need another app that emulates old video terminals.

If you haven't used the Terminal app in your Mac or Windows Terminal in your Windows operating system, **you still can recognize the typical black screen with green fonts that the hackers in the movies use** to quickly type commands instead of using a mouse or trackpad.

Once a user is in the terminal, the interaction between the user and system is line by line—hence its name. The terminal prompts waiting for instructions, the user types a command and pushes enter, and the terminal responds with the result.

Several things have changed in the new terminal apps depending on the operating system and the version—like the commands, a richer design, and the ways to interact with it—but they are still text-based interfaces very similar to Unix.

For example, in Unix, if you typed and send the command "date" on the terminal, then the system *printed* the current date in the next line.

On one hand, you have a system function that prints the date, and on the other hand, you have a command to execute the function. The name of the command should reflect the function to make it easy to recall. The function is "date" and we call it by the command "date". **Sounds easy, right?**

In the old systems, you always had a problem with the memory capacity of the machine, hence the use of abbreviations for the commands.

The trouble with Unix in 1981

One of the most relevant critiques of Don Norman to the Unix user interface was the lack of consistency. For example, to change a password you typed "passwd". To copy you typed "cp". They look easy to recall but there was no consistency in the number of characters or the way they were constructed.

In some cases, you use two characters of the function name, in others the first ones, and in others, you use the consonants. **Zero consistency.**

To open the editor app you typed "ed". Once open, you could write on it whatever text you were working on. To close the editor, you typed the command "q" (you guessed it, an abbreviation of "quit") and the editor quitted... without saving your work and without any warning that your text was going to be lost.

A little exegesis of the text

I found two versions of the article written by Don Norman. The final version was published in *Datamation* — scanned from the original — and a version was uploaded directly by Norman himself. It looks like the latest was the final draft previously to be edited by the magazine. **Some differences are worth noting.**

The title of the original version was 'The truth about Unix: The user interface is horrid'. The published version softened it to 'The Trouble with Unix', and added the much less aggressive running head 'The system design is elegant but the user interface is not'.

The last paragraph in the original version closed with:

"Treat the user with intelligence. There is no need to talk down to the user, nor to explain everything. But give the user a share in understanding by presenting a consistent view of the system."

The final version eliminated the reference to user intelligence and added:

"But give the users a share in understanding by presenting a consistent view of the system. Their response will be your reward."

Datamation also added two boxed texts in the magazine, one titled "What is Unix?", it's a helpful explanation for the novice, and the other titled "Another view", which is the anticipated reply from Michael Lesk, the Unix developer.

These are important remarks because **you can see the extreme precautions the editors took with an article** that dared to point out the errors of the best operating system designed to date.

The origin and growth of a revolutionary idea

Other takeaways for those like me who love to see how ideas are born and grown are some of the condensed insights that the father of user experience design wrote. **You can see the origin of what he proposed later in his foundational books and papers about user experience design.**

The thing that marvels me too is how these ideas were thought of with a text-based user interface in mind. We are so used to thinking about an interface as graphics-based that it amuses me **how Norman could begin composing his principles by thinking about words, characters, line-by-line interactions, and so on.**

> *"System designers take note. Design the system for the person, not for the computer, not even for yourself."* — Don Norman

In some way, **the first computer UX design ideas were more what we call today UX writing than UI design** — considering that when you hear or read UI design you usually think of a graphic user interface. What Don Norman was doing in the article is what you expect today from a UX writer.

Just with the recent massive use of smart speakers and assistants, we are coming back to a text-based interface and the subsequent design of them. I wonder if the previous use of command-line interfaces gives me some advantage in understanding how Alexa, Siri, or Cortana work, in juxtaposition to the trouble my wife and daughter — who haven't used a CLI — have with them.

Let me finish quoting five jewels from the article, but I really recommend you to read it yourself. This selection is free of criticism and irony and collects positive suggestions and propositions. And remember, **they were written in 1981, seven years before the original "The Design of Everyday Things".**

· "People are complex entities and can adapt to almost anything. As a result, designers often design for themselves,

without regard for other kinds of users."
- "Users develop mental models of the devices with which they interact. If you do not provide them with one, they will make one up themselves, and the one they create is apt to be wrong."
- "Feedback is of critical importance, both in helping to establish the appropriate mental model and in letting the user keep its current state in synchrony with the actual system."
- "System designers take note. Design the system for the person, not for the computer, not even for yourself."
- "People are also information processing systems, with varying degrees of knowledge, varying degrees of experience."

References

I leave the references to the end with the intention to hide the name of the article's author at the beginning and keep some suspense for entertainment purposes, but you will find everything in the next links.

- The truth about Unix Don Norman[102]. The published article in 1981 by *Datamation*.
- The trouble with UNIX: The user interface is horrid[103]. The original version before being edited.

---

[102] Donald A., Norman. "The Truth about Unix: The User Interface Is Horrid." *Datamation*, 1981. http://www.ceri.memphis.edu/people/smalley/ESCI720 5_misc_files/The_truth_about_Unix_cleaned.pdf.

[103] Norman, Donald. "The Trouble with UNIX: The User Interface Is Horrid." *Datamation* 27 (January 1, 1981): 139–50.

· Where Did the Term "User Experience" Come From?[104] on Adobe Blog.
· Who are the founders of UX Design? at UX Collective.[105]

[104] Lyonnais, Sheena. "Where Did the Term 'User Experience' Come From?" Adobe Blog. Accessed May 25, 2023. https://blog.adobe.com/en/publish/2017/08/28/where-did-the-term-user-experience-come-from.

[105] Green, Taylor. "Who Are the Founders of UX Design?" Medium, September 25, 2018. https://uxdesign.cc/who-are-the-founding-fathers-of-ux-design-e41158dbc6e5.

21

The 3 most important skills at work

For designers, developers, project and product managers, working at the office or working from home

Do designers have to know how to program? Do programmers have to know how to design? Do you need a general vision but without leaving attention to details? The intuition of what the user wants or needs? Discipline? Willingness to learn? Experience? Social skills?

These are the 3 most important skills at work according to my experience. And I have worked for small and large companies; old-established ones, as well as startups; manufacturing, services, content, or development-oriented; and I, have been in several positions in different areas. Let's see.

1. Writing

Writing is a way to organize tasks, ideas, and requirements. Most of what you write may never be read by your coworkers, clients, or boss, but it's fundamental to keep you organized anyway.

The most basic job in any office or work needs self-organization skills. That is accomplished with writing.

Writing is remembering. Our brain memorizes better what you do — active learning — than what you read or think — passive learning. That's why when you write an idea or a task you may not need to check it again. You just remember it.

In some cases like me, once I write an idea or task I remember it better even without looking at the words I wrote. I even remember where I wrote it — not just on which paper but on what part of the page. If you are a visual person like me, writing is not about just words but ideas on a surface.

Writing is planning. Visualizing a calendar, a waterfall chart, a Gantt chart, a Kanban board, an organigram, a timeline... And even other more text-based forms like changelogs, roadmaps, release notes, and readme files, have an inherent visual and space organization that supports planning and organizing.

Some people or some professions need different kinds of support for writing: notebooks, legal pads, whiteboards, cardboards, post-its, flip charts... And these days we have a lot of digital tools to help us with these tasks. But no matter if you use Trello or Asana, Slack or Teams, Confluence or Sharepoint, all these great tools are useless if they are empty. They need text.

2. Writing

Writing is the most important way of communication in any work. No matter if you use modern videoconferences systems, in the end, everybody needs a written minute.

Or no matter how visual is your work, even graphics, libraries, or prototypes need text and comments for context and understanding. User stories or requirements can be illustrated, but they are narrated mainly in text form. Any questions, comments, or afterwords to them must be in written form also.

Emails and chats can be expressive with the support of emojis or gifs. Or they can be used to embed images, documents, or files. But again, in the end, the text is key.

Communication includes presentations and training. No matter if they are traditional PowerPoints or more of a TedTalk-like style, you need to write at least an outline. If the presentation is in collaboration, text notes are fundamental. And in the end, people need a takeaway in the form of text.

Some online collaboration documents look great because they make us think that we can share a presentation or a document and avoid writing explanations. I'm talking about Google Docs, Evernote, Dropbox Paper, Notion... But all of them come with a comment or notes system, and if you have tried to use them with someone, you already know how much you need to keep everything written down to avoid misunderstandings.

Decades ago, we had shorthand or tachygraphy, a system to write fast and briefly with the use of symbols and abbreviations. It was very common for secretaries and office assistants — and even some executives — to learn shorthand besides typing. A boss called the secretary to dictate to her a letter, for example, and she could write down her or his words without the need to stop her or stop him. Then the same secretary transcribed the shorthand to paper through the typing machine.

Today, there is no need for that. In every work, it's expected that the employers can type no matter the speed. Nobody asks you in a job interview if you can use a keyboard. It's implicit. If the job really requires specialization, they may ask you for your words-per-minute record but that it's very strange.

Writing is knowledge, and knowledge in an organization is an asset. With a good documentation system, any new employee can learn what was done before and avoid repeating mistakes. Any company can shoot down a project or a line of production area and restart it again later based on the documentation.

3. Writing

Writing is thinking. This is a skill that is overlooked by most professionals. When you need to clarify an idea or you don't know how to solve a problem you can write it down. Do you remember how do you solve a math problem? You have to write down the elements of the equation, and identify the expressions, terms, variables, constants...

"A problem defined is half-solved", my math teacher used to say. And to define, you need to write it down.

And writing is drawing too. We are used to thinking in writing just as words on paper but drawing, diagramming, dribbling, doodling, and sketching have been part of the general concept of "writing" for a very long time.

Leonardo DaVinci's Notebooks or Galileo Galilei's papers are some of the most famous examples of this, but you can look for the manuscripts of different scientists, artists, and writers. Writing on paper escapes linearity and it's very common to find little notes, and comments, some of them circled or lined in the handwritten notes of them.

(Go and search for Steve Jobs[106]*,* Bill Gates[107]*, or* Jony Ive[108] *handwritten and manuscripts notes. I can't use them here for Copywrite reasons, but they are worth watching.)*

Writing as an extension of our thoughts has been a challenge for software developers since the beginning of the computer. Today you can find very diverse apps with this intention: Workflowy, Org-Mode, Roam Research, DEVONthink, Tinderbox, personal wikis... Great apps and systems that need writing.

Writing is learning also. Current jobs need professionals that can learn fast. The best way to learn is through writing. There are several ways to take notes to study a subject, but against what some can think, reading isn't enough. You have to write. You can take notes, make flashcards, mind maps, glossaries, diagrams... In the end, you have to write to learn.

Writing, writing, and writing

So, the 3 most important skills at work are writing, writing, and writing. Every rule has its exceptions, of course.

I can guess that someone is going to say that s/he doesn't write and hasn't needed it in her or his work.

Another one is going to say that in her or his business, they don't need to write everything down because they use X or Y

---

[106] "Steve Jobs Handwriting Notes - Google Search." Accessed May 25, 2023. https://www.google.com/search?q=steve+jobs+handwriting+notes.

[107] "Bill Gates Handwriting Notes - Google Search." Accessed May 25, 2023. https://www.google.com/search?q=bill+gates+handwriting+notes.

[108] "Jony Ive Handwriting Notebook - Google Search." Accessed May 25, 2023. https://www.google.com/search?q=jony+ive+handwriting+notebook.

visual system or tool.

One more is going to say that s/he knows a professional that doesn't write very well but because s/he is very good at her or his work that doesn't matter.

As I said, exceptions apply. But I ask you to think again about those exceptions. I have been in businesses that don't like to write, especially to keep documentation. But as soon as someone leaves, whoever arrives for replacement has to learn everything from zero because there is no knowledge stored in documents, wikis, or any other system.

And I have met good designers and developers that don't like to write, just design and code. This has happened in small companies. As soon as they are in a large one or the one they are in has grown, they start suffering because no matter how good their design or code nobody else can follow their decisions and reasons to work in one way instead of another.

Even in the simple things. I remember having designers or developers that have big problems writing an email to ask for access to a server, an account, a license, or even to request a new computer or a desk.

So, in short, you can avoid writing at work. But if you are there for the long run, don't put aside the importance of writing.

Further reading

- Ad Aged: Good writing is a business advantage.[109]
- Bad Writing Is Destroying Your Company's Productivity[110].
- Always Be Journaling—Letters To A New Developer[111].
- How to Master All the Hows to Write—The Writing Cooperative[112].
- How to Use the Conjecture Method for Your Writing—The Startu[113]p.
- How to Rewire Your Brain to Make Your Writing Flow—The Writing Cooperative[114].

[109] Tannenbaum, George. "Ad Aged: Good Writing Is a Business Advantage. (An Advertisement for Myself.)." *Ad Aged* (blog), April 13, 2020. http://ada ged.blogspot.com/2020/04/good-writing-is-business-advantage.html.

[110] Bernoff, Josh. "Bad Writing Is Destroying Your Company's Productivity." *Harvard Business Review*, September 6, 2016. https://hbr.org/2016/09/bad-writing-is-destroying-your-companys-productivity.

[111] mooreds. "Always Be Journaling." *Letters To A New Developer* (blog), December 14, 2018. https://letterstoanewdeveloper.com/2018/12/14/alwa ys-be-journaling/.

[112] Corona, Adolfo Ramírez. "How to Master All the Hows to Write." Medium, January 17, 2020. https://writingcooperative.com/how-to-master-all-th e-hows-to-write-cd9013aa2069.

[113] Corona, Adolfo Ramírez. "How to Use the Conjecture Method for Your Writing." *The Startup* (blog), January 30, 2020. https://medium.com/swlh/ how-to-use-the-conjecture-method-for-your-writing-5c687f47b381.

[114] Corona, Adolfo Ramírez. "How to Rewire Your Brain to Make Your Writing Flow." Medium, March 9, 2020. https://writingcooperative.com/how-to-rewire-your-brain-to-make-your-writing-flow-564ccbbbe50c.

IV

On objects and products

22

Paper: the unavoidable interface

I was wrong. We all were wrong

In this digital era, what do you think is the life expectancy of technology like paper notepads? Do you dream of a future with a simple "Alexa, take note of this"? Or you are in search of a frictionless way of taking notes or capturing text?

What if I tell you that the expected life expectancy of paper notepads in our daily lives is longer than an iPad, not to say "Alexa"?

iPads have been around in the face of the Earth for only a little more than ten years. Alexa is just a newborn in the tech world.

Paper notebooks have been with us for at least six hundred years.

The Lindy effect is a concept that says the older a technology is, the longer is likely to be around in the future. Under this idea, it's more probable that we'll still see and use paper notebooks in the next hundred years than iPads or Alexas.

The dream that never was

The dream was born with the rise of the personal computer. In the nineteen seventies with the appearance of computer screens and digitalization, the idea of a paperless office began to form in some companies and businesses.

Of course, there was a big reduction in the use of paper in almost every industry, but nothing close to "paperless". Some areas in some businesses even started to print more — it was easier thanks to the printer.

(One of the arguments in favor of a paperless office was to save trees from being converted into paper. The problem is that the production of electronic devices — in the amount that the current consumption demands — comes with a big carbon footprint.)

Personally, I must admit that when I bought a Palm Pilot — a very old handheld PC — around the year two thousand, I thought the same: a world without paper, a world without capturing or digitalizing the physical or analog world.

I was wrong. We all were wrong.

The unavoidable advantages

Paper notebooks, notepads, legal or yellow pads, journals, and sketchbooks... have technological advantages that iPads, tablets, iPhones, smartphones, or smartwatches, don't have.

- Cheap: really, really cheap.
- Simple: you can use notepads as examples of simplicity.

- High resolution at a low cost: have you seen the beauty of a 0.15 mm black ink line on blank paper?
- Wide types of input encodings: text, math symbols, drawings, vectors, images...
- No batteries: no cords or power source either.
- Open source "software" and hardware technology: anyone can make them, and anyone can use them
- Age-less technology: I can open one of my old notebooks from the last years of the previous century and use it as time hasn't passed; try that with a Palm Pilot.
- Fast responsiveness: to begin with, you don't need to put your fingerprint or passcode, but more than that, jotting things down is faster on paper.

The note-taking brain

But the most important advantage of paper notebooks against digital ones or note-taking apps is related to how your brain is activated in the process. In this domain, paper notebooks have more advantages.

New technics to optimize memorization and learning, like the very trendy spaced repetition system, lack what simple handwriting things down does with your brain:

- Enables the summarization and reframing of information in your own handwritten words for encoding.
- Handwriting is a very active visual and tactile task: you have to perceive constant physical sizes and spatial locations — paper provides physical, tactile, and spatiotemporally references to the text.
- The use of paper enhances the experience of writing adding

163

episodic and spatial information to it: thinking and learning begins in the sensory-motor system and is based on
reference frames.

Questions for learning

So, these are my questions — the kind of questions previous to
experimentation.

- The paperless future never arrived — analog and digital
  writing systems coexist. How can we have the best of both
  worlds?
- What analog tools — paper-based writing or drawing systems — should be part of what you do for work, study, or a
  hobby?
- What are the pros and cons of still using them? Do they
  still have value? How to integrate them into your digital
  daily life?

These questions are behind the course Writing on Paper in
the Digital Age where we'll review an inventory of mediums,
techniques, tools, and workflows for writing in both, the analog
and digital world, contrast them with how each of us uses
them, and consider alternatives to improve our daily writing
practices.

What I would like is to identify and recognize which analog
tools and workflows are still useful in our digital life and design
a better integration of both.

References:

- 4 Reasons Writing Things Down on Paper Still Reigns Supreme | Psychology Today[115]
- Frontiers | Paper Notebooks vs. Mobile Devices: Brain Activation Differences During Memory Retrieval | Behavioral Neuroscience[116]
- A Thousand Brains: A New Theory Of Intelligence by Jeff Hawkins[117]

(Published on Mar 22, 2021, in Medium)

---

[115] "4 Reasons Writing Things Down on Paper Still Reigns Supreme | Psychology Today." Accessed May 25, 2023. https://www.psychologytoday.com/us/blog/the-athletes-way/202103/4-reasons-writing-things-down-paper-still-reigns-supreme.

[116] Umejima, Keita, Takuya Ibaraki, Takahiro Yamazaki, and Kuniyoshi L. Sakai. "Paper Notebooks vs. Mobile Devices: Brain Activation Differences During Memory Retrieval." *Frontiers in Behavioral Neuroscience* 15 (2021). https://www.frontiersin.org/articles/10.3389/fnbeh.2021.634158.

[117] Numenta. "A Thousand Brains: A New Theory Of Intelligence by Jeff Hawkins." Accessed May 25, 2023. https://www.numenta.com/resources/books/a-thousand-brains-by-jeff-hawkins/.

23

The best second display you may ever find as a designer

And 6 reasons to radically change the way you work at your desk

I remember when we used to work on a desk. We used to have notebooks, paper reports, printed faxes, books, post-its, a calculator, a ruler, pens, pencils... Our work area was big. We had several documents opened at the same time.

Well, a little chaos helps with creativity, right?

Yes, I'm old. I'm talking about the pre-PC era. Designers and visual artists used to have a drawing table where they planned, drew, or even made physical prototypes.

At some moments in my life, I have done some drawing and illustrations but not enough to consider buying a drawing table. Anyway, I always adored the idea of having all that large space to work. One of these days, perhaps.

166

The trend of a multi-monitor workspace

At the beginning of the personal computer revolution, the idea to have a second monitor was unthinkable because of the costs and the size of the monitors.

As you know, today it's very common for programmers to have at least two monitors. One for the code and the other for the rest — email, messages, web surfing, references, or testing.

Instead, most of the designers I know prefer the large screen over a second monitor — or just a little one aside.

I have used two monitors myself, one for the occasional HTML or CSS code to check, and the other, like the programmers, for the rest of the apps, testing, and documents.

In my experience, it's very useful to have a couple of screens to separate writing long pieces of text from other operational daily tasks, for example.

Having your main project in one monitor allows you to have a better focus on it, avoid distractions, and help your brain switch contexts — every time you turn to see a monitor your brain connects with the project on it.

In a lot of offices, you still find drawing tables or spaces to work apart from the computer. But most of the work is digital.

You can work on very large monitors or have more than one to try to match the space of those drawing tables from the past. Dual or multiple monitor setups, ultrawide screens, curved displays...

But, let's face it, there are a lot of disadvantages to working on large or second monitors:

- You never stop focusing on a screen, no matter how big or how many. Being in focus looks to be a thing these days, but we have to be careful not to misunderstand the value of focusing on one task with having your sight in one place.

- They use a lot of space in your work area, even if you hang the monitors on the wall or on a stand designed for that purpose.
- If you have a laptop, it's great to have a bigger or a second monitor at the office or home, but of course, that second monitor is not portable.
- The quality of the image resolution, the light, and even the colors make any modern monitor benign for your eyes. But no matter if it's a monitor, a blackboard, or a wall, staring for too long periods in one place is not good for your eyes.
- They consume a lot of energy, especially if you use them to their full capacity.
- Sometimes one monitor for just reading a web page or just looking at it when a new message or email arrives can be too much.

A hybrid solution: screen + paper

For me, the best second display is not LCD, LED, or plasma but a paper-based display: a notebook, a notepad, a journal, or even sheets of paper.

I'm not being cheap. I think there are a lot of advantages to having a paper-based workspace next to your computer.

1. It's good for your brain to switch contexts beyond the computer monitor. Forget augmented or virtual reality, keeping notes, to-do lists, ideas, sketches, diagrams, or mind maps on paper allows your brain to locate things in a three-dimensional environment.

168

2. The paper display can be as small or as large as you want. The kind and color of the paper it's up to you also. I like plain paper because I can have notes and ideas but also sketches or diagrams. And a notebook allows me to open it and have the space of a page or a double page depending on my needs at the moment.

3. You can change your input tool. No matter if you use words or images, occasionally leave the keyboard, and the mouse or trackpad, and give some rest to your body from a fixed position.

4. Like you, I have used that photo editing or drawing app for hours to be on time for a deadline. After that, I have dreamed of designing on that screen when going to bed. Yes, I have dreamed of nodes and Bézier curves. You can change your point of view or your perspective about your project using two different tools, one digital and another analog.

5. Changing focus and looking to a different surface for your words or images is good for your eyes.

6. Your paper-based workspace is portable. You can carry it and use it next to your laptop at the cafe.

There is more

One of the unsuspecting advantages of a second analog display is that it can be your main workspace and not your second.

When I need to outline, diagram, or draw a concept map for a project, I work better on paper. I make more space for the notepad — or a simple sheet of paper — on my desk and leave the computer monitor to the side. I might still use the screen to look for something on the web or read an opened document, but for several minutes my main work is done on paper.

A sheet of paper can become my drawing or mindmap app, my canvas, my workspace, my text editor... sometimes even my spreadsheet.

I'm not against electronic displays. Even if you already have a large or second monitor, having a paper-based workspace can help you. You may have Post-Its or little notebooks, but what I propose is to do part of your work on paper, parallel to your work on the screen.

Do you need to have everything on the cloud for reference or to share it with co-workers? A photo with your smartphone can be enough but there are many apps to keep handmade sketches or manuscripts on the cloud.

I invite you to try it. How does a paper-based workspace function for you?

(Published on Mar 3, 2020, in UX Collective)

24

What does a smartphone smell like?

The human experience lives in three dimensions. All Design Is 3D Design

The actual digital graphic design process lives in wireframes, prototypes, mockups, user flow diagrams, site maps...

But every human experience—ergo, every user experience—lives in three dimensions.

When the final product of your design is going to be a 3D object, the design process contemplates a 3D visualization of its potential use in three dimensions, necessarily.

But when the final product of your design is going to be a 2D object (like an app for a screen or a printed material) the design process usually visualizes the two dimensions of the plane: the eye travel on the surface and (in the case of the app) the touch interactions of the finger.

But never forget that the two-dimensional world is just an abstraction. No objects are living in two dimensions. Except for those living in the imaginary Flatland.

The old times

We used to design in 2D only one stage of the complete process of design.

We used to draw sketches, diagrams, planes, or blueprints, but that was only one part of what we did to give birth to a product.

I remember that even when we used to design something on the screen of our computer, we used to print it "to see how it looks". I don't see that very often anymore.

Or, do you remember the color proofs or cromalin? Or what about the dummy print?

Today, sometimes the whole design process of digital products lives in 2D.

Yes, we have layers, levels, shadows, and even skeuomorphic elements, to give some appearance of a three-dimensional space.

But that's not what I'm talking about.

Remember, the user doesn't use a product. The user experiences a product.

What's experience? A little bit of Psychology

Let's get out of the design world and go to the psychological world.

We used to talk about "user experience". I'm a psychotherapist, besides my work in software and systems projects, so "experience" has an extra layer of meaning.

Experience[118] is what you actually live through, in contrast to what you imagine or think. You are conscious of what you experience. The experience is the content of your consciousness.

For example, you went sailing a sailboat or climbing a mountain. After, you tell your friends that it's difficult to describe the event because you have to live it, to *experience* it by yourself.

In some philosophical and psychological schools of thought, consciousness and experience are the same or at least, overlap in features.

> *...we have [experiencial] states when we see, hear, smell, taste and have pains."*
>
> *[Experiential properties are] ...sensations, feelings and perceptions, but I would also include thoughts, wants and emotions—Ned Block*[119]*, On a Confusion about a Function of Consciousness*[120]*.*

So you don't imagine or think of an experience. You have to actually live it with all your senses and be conscious of that.

---

[118] "APA Dictionary of Psychology." Accessed May 25, 2023. https://dictionar y.apa.org/.

[119] "Ned Block." In *Wikipedia*, October 10, 2022. https://en.wikipedia.org/w/ index.php?title=Ned_Block&oldid=1115200729.

[120] "ON A CONFUSION ABOUT A FUNCTION OF CONSCIOUSNESS." Accessed May 25, 2023. https://web-archive.southampton.ac.uk/cogprints.org/231/ 1/199712004.html.

Experience in design

Back to the design world. Let me translate (or transpose) these definitions to the user experience.

The user experience of any product is in a state where he sees, hears, smells, tastes, and has pains.

The properties of his experience are sensations, feelings, perceptions, thoughts, wants, and emotions.

When you present a digital product to a user, there are aspects of his experiential state that are out of your control. But that doesn't mean they are not going to happen.

In principle, you can't control what the user is going to smell when using your app. Your app doesn't smell, but your app is going to be on a smartphone.

What does a smartphone smell like?

A thought experiment

Let's imagine you are designing a medical app for patients that need nutritional menus. Let's say some of those patients are recovering from cancer treatment, like chemotherapy.

Are you going to include color photos of the dishes? It may look like a 2D question. The photos may look nice in an aesthetical o compositional way.

But, is the app going to be used in a Hospital? Is the patient going to be smelling and tasting the sequels of chemotherapy? What does he is going to be feeling at the moment of seeing nutritional tips? What are going to be his thoughts, wants or emotions?

Does the idea to include full-color food photos look promising when you visualize the complete experience of the user?

Does that is going to be in the mood of a cancer patient? Those look like 3D questions.

Yes, this is a very specific case. But I'm using it to make my point.

Two car examples

The first time I used Waze I was driving. I mean, not the first time I *opened* the app, but the first time I *used* it. It was a very bad experience. It was obvious to me that there were graphical elements whose functions were very difficult to access if you were driving. In the first versions of the app that wasn't put into consideration.

Now, when you open the app there is a message that says you can't use the app if you are driving. Good to know!

Waze is a 3D experience that needs a 3D process design.

Adding to the car experience. How many people use airplane mode on their smartphones and how frequently?

There are too many more people that use to drive a car and more frequently. But, I haven't seen the car mode button in a more accessible place than the airplane mode button on a smartphone.

The airplane mode in smartphones was designed to comply with airplane requirements, not user requirements.

A car mode or driving mode is a function or element to comply with the user experience.

Outside of any user flow diagram: escaping Flatland

We have to escape Flatland (Edward Tufte's sculptures and chapter's book reference intended[121]).

You can design multiple user flow diagrams or travel user experiences. Most of the time this includes only the travel of flow through the app we are designing.

But a smartphone or tablet is not a single app device. In the middle of any moment of the experience, the user can switch to another app, be interrupted by another app, or leave the entire phone — ergo, the app — and go to his 3D world.

Is the user going to find everything in the same place he left the app when he came back? Does he need to come back to the same place or need a resume?

I use Google News once in a while on my smartphone. In the middle of reviewing my news feed, I have to change to another app or another activity outside my phone. I come back to the app a few minutes later. Maybe more than I thought because the app just refreshes all my news feeds and I lose track of my previous review.

I haven't used Facebook for a while but I think the same happens there.

On more than one occasion I tried to open my Starbucks app to pay for my coffee just to discover that I was logged out from the app. I have to write my entire email again and my secure passcode on the little screen of my cellphone — caps, small caps, numbers, special characters — while other people are waiting

---

[121] "Edward Tufte Forum: Escaping Flatland Sculptures." Accessed May 25, 2023. https://www.edwardtufte.com/bboard/q-and-a-fetch-msg?msg_id=0002Oo.

in line behind me. Not a good experience.

Remember

1. When designing, leave your screen once in a while. The screen, apps, and tools you are using on your computer are just part of the design process. You have to live, to experience the design itself.
2. Exercise visualization. Not just with user flow diagrams but visualizing the living and experience of the user. Even your 2D design is going to be an object in the 3D experience of your user.
3. The map is not the territory. You have to continuously update your maps with the data that only the territory can give you.
4. Don't overestimate the power of imagination. Fiction writers used to do field trips to the locations of the stories they write because reality gives them elements their imagination can't.
5. The prototype, testing and iterating stages have to be done with real users. And the users have to use the apps in real scenarios. It's very common to aisle the user's tests removing variables like incoming phone calls. The real user is going to receive a phone call, eventually.

(Published on Nov 5, 2019, in UX Collective)

25

If your product was a song, could you hum its hook?

Things product designers can learn from songwriting

A product is like a song: it needs a hook.

Let's talk about hooks in songwriting and what a product or experience designer can learn from them.

Not to be confused with the "hook model[122]" to catch and hold habits in your customers, or with the marketing hook[123] used in slogans or taglines.

---

[122] Vinod, Hari. "Making Your Product A Habit: The Hook Framework." *Medium* (blog), December 30, 2018. https://medium.com/@svharivinod/making-your-product-a-habit-the-hook-framework-7815f94a2ddf.

[123] Small Business - Chron.com. "What Is a Hook in Marketing?" Accessed May 25, 2023. https://smallbusiness.chron.com/hook-marketing-34667.html.

What is a 'hook' in a song?

Every song needs what musicians call "the hook", a short riff or phrase, that sticks in our mind — the verse we repeat again and again.

The hook stands out and is easily remembered. When good, a hook makes the success of a song even if the rest isn't as good as the hook itself.

Let's make a little exercise. Do you recognize these hooks?:

- "Stop! In the name of love".
- "Call me maybe".
- "Sweet Caroline".
- "I will survive".
- "Good, good, good! Good vibrations".
- "Under Pressure".
- "Ah ah ah ah, stayin' alive, stayin' alive".
- "Dancing queen".
- "I Want to Hold Your Hand".

You might not remember the name of the song, the composer, or even the singer, but you recognize the hook in a song.

In terms of composition, a song sustains the hook and works for the hook. You want to make the hook look clear and high. The rest of the elements don't have to distract the attention of the listener from the hook but take her or take him to it.

And maybe the most important characteristic of a hook is that it brings an emotional experience to the listener.

The hook in product design

Every product is the same. You need a hook. Especially in new products. Something that makes your product different from the other products in its category.

Gmail wasn't the first free webmail service but, in the beginning, offered almost free unlimited memory storage (do you remember the subtle text reminder of how many gigabytes you had?).

When the first **iPod** was launched there were other music players, but the hook was clear: "1,000 songs in your pocket."

And what about **Google Search**? Not the first web search engine but the first to search for text within web pages and documents.

It should be easy to find and identify (discoverability and understanding, again) but also it should be something in the product (an interaction or function) that the user is constantly using.

In the case of **Coca-Cola** was the container: a "bottle so distinct that you would recognize if by feel in the dark or lying broken on the ground.[124]"

The hook for your product might work with the marketing of it. It can be a slogan or tagline.

The **M&M** chocolates have a hard candy cover: "melts in your mouth, not in your hands".

Or the famous size and shape of the original **Volkswagen Beetle** and its slogan "Think small".

---

[124] "The History of the Coca-Cola Contour Bottle - News & Articles." Accessed May 25, 2023. https://www.coca-colacompany.com/about-us/history/th e-history-of-the-coca-cola-contour-bottle.

Sometimes the product constraints for the user can be a way to highlight the hook.

Twitter's 140-character restriction allowed posting from SMS messaging but it was also in sync with the name:

> *"a short burst of inconsequential information," and*
> *"chirps from birds."* —*Jack Dorsey*[125]

Instagram only allowed squared photos with 640 pixels of resolution at the beginning so you could share them with anyone, no matter the cellphone model.

Starbucks doesn't have a delivery service because you have to live the experience in the store.

The hook in **Hotmail** was the main feature of the product: free webmail "and the ability to access a user's inbox from anywhere in the world[126]." ISP mail had a lot of advantages over webmail but was not relevant for the common user.

All the design of your product has to work for the hook—at least, as I said, at the launch. You can't have several hooks. You need only one and all the elements of the product should work for it.

The hook makes a promise about a product and the product has to keep it.

Apple Newton was the first personal digital assistant, technologically advanced and innovative. But there were two

---

[125] Los Angeles Times. "Twitter Creator Jack Dorsey Illuminates the Site's Founding Document. Part I," February 19, 2009. https://www.latimes.com/archives/blogs/technology-blog/story/2009-02-18/twitter-creator-jack-dorsey-illuminates-the-sites-founding-document-part-i.

[126] "Outlook.Com." In *Wikipedia*, May 20, 2023. https://en.wikipedia.org/w/index.php?title=Outlook.com&oldid=1156047538.

main problems with it. One of the hooks was its handwriting recognition feature, and it didn't deliver. The other was that it has several ambiguous hooks for the time: notes, contacts, agenda, calculator, conversion calculators, and time-zone maps... under the name of personal data and organization management. It was everything.

Part of the technology and ideas in the **Apple Newton** were used on the **iPhone** — this one with a good hook: a smartphone with a multi-touch screen. The rest of the applications on the device were to be gradually discovered by the user.

As in song composition, sometimes you have the song and you need a hook. But other times, you have the hook and need the rest of the song.

PlayStation is a great product, but that iconic dual analog controller made a difference to other game consoles.

There were social networks before **Facebook**, but the feature to "find your friends" was a good hook, especially because you could find old friends — thanks to that **Facebook** was one of the first to ask for your email to sign up.

A product can be useful and help or serve the consumer, but if it doesn't have a hook it can be difficult to deliver.

Tinder wasn't the first online dating service, but swiping to like or dislike was a very good hook for a mobile app.

"All You Need Is Love"

And what about the most important characteristic of a hook?

There is no better example of a company that delivers an emotional experience in its products than **Disney**. Imagination, dreams, fantasy, happiness... "remember it was all started by a mouse".

Not for nothing, Walt Disney has been considered the first UX designer[127].

What do you think? Can you identify the hook for other products? Does your product have a hook?

Or do you simply have a favorite hook from a song?

(Published on Feb 19, 2020, in UX Collective)

---

[127] Parker, Elias. "Walt Disney: The World's First UX Designer." UX Magazine, September 9, 2013. https://uxmag.com/articles/walt-disney-the-worlds-first-ux-designer.

26

All products have unintended side effects: which have yours?

Some can be innovative and disruptive; others can be adverse for your users or your product itself

When you design a product or service and the experience associated with it, there are side effects or side experiences secondary to the one intended.

Side effects can be small or big, beneficial or adverse, intentional or unintentional, expected or unexpected. Some can be neither beneficial nor adverse, just neutral.

The unintentional and unexpected side effects of a product or service design can be particularly important to the grade of radical change or even create new experiences or new behaviors.

Let's see some cases.

Beneficial or neutral side effects

The release of all the episodes of a TV series on streaming services like Netflix brought the phenomenon of binge TV, a side effect that became an experience itself.

With the design of the TV remote control, the side effect was TV zapping—a phenomenon itself, a new behavior, a new experience.

With the design of a search engine like Google to find more relevant information on the web, you might not anticipate an interface to the biggest human knowledge database in history and the subsequent googling experience of "ask anything".

Adverse side effects

But in other cases, the side effects are adverse. Tobacco and cigarettes are the archetypal old example, but smartphones and digital addiction are other new ones.

Fake news is not always intentional. Fake news sometimes is the consequence of fast news[128]. The possibility of instant publishing and distribution of content comes with it the easily spread of unreliable information.

Most of the actual problems of cities and urban planning come from unintended experiences derived from urban policies. Sometimes they are just bad designs under political or commercial interests. But others are a product of good intentions.

For instance, cars and streets brought the side effects of

---

[128] Corona, Adolfo Ramírez. "Fast News or the Death of a Celebrity." *Medium* (blog), March 10, 2018. https://adolforismos.medium.com/fast-news-or-the-death-of-a-celebrity-93cb7354a8e.

pollution and traffic. And you may think that this side effect was evident, but it wasn't in the beginning.

If you think the solution to cars in cities is bikes, just google "china bicycle traffic[129]" and watch the images to see the side effects of that solution. There are also side effects for scooters.[130]

Amazon's book recommendations sounded great at the beginning. Based on your previous purchases, searches, and what other readers have bought, they show you books you may like.

Or googling for a specialized physician when you are sick and getting results near where you are, it's an undoubted advantage for a product and your experience with it.

But today, almost everybody is concerned about the side effects of customized search results —privacy, tracking practices, and the potential misuse and abuse of your personal data.

Preventing side effects

With digital products, you can start with a *minimum viable product* (MVP) and repetitively iterate development and deployment. You can start to see unintended side effects from the first iterations and make corrections.

In physical products, it is not as easy as in the digital world, but you can manage batch production with a progressive escalation—producing small batches and making corrections

---

[129] "China Bicycle Traffic - Google Search." Accessed May 25, 2023. https://www.google.com/search?q=china+bicycle+traffic.

[130] Guerra, Joseph. "Scooters to Cities as Features to Products." Medium, October 3, 2018. https://uxdesign.cc/scooters-to-cities-as-features-to-products-32f8dbf3893a.

in the next ones.

Just consider this, whether digital or physical. Some side effects just appear after an inflection point in time or scale — after a long time of adoption or massive use.

A social network needs a lot of users to see its benefits and, as recent history has shown us, a lot more to see its unintended effects.

The limits of predictive models

You can't build a model to predict side effects derived from time or scale.

There are several reasons for that, but one of the most important is that you can't model a system based on a model. Well, you can but your margin of error increases.

In other words, we can make assumptions with a "what if" statement—to model possible future scenarios. That is reasonable and useful.

And after that, we can nest "what if" statements inside others. But remember the result of the first "what if" statement is a hypothesis, so when you make a new "what if" statement based on a hypothesis you start to chain assumptions, not facts. Hypothesis based on hypothesis. That's mere speculation.

There are side effects or unintended experiences that are unpredictable because of uncertainty.

You don't avoid side effects. You should be always aware of possible side effects and learn or correct them if necessary.

TV zapping changed the way TV was produced and programmed. Before, you had a captive audience that watched a TV program from start to end. With the arrival of the remote and an easy way to change channels, TV created more

187

WHEN I GROW UP I WANT TO BE A UX DESIGNER, DAD

attractive segments or time blocks to keep the attention and avoid zapping[131].

Old movies, made for theaters, have a slow and long introduction to characters and situations. In a theater, you can't change channels.

But later on, movies made with the intention to be released on TV after the box office began to use the "start with action, explain later" formula that works better for an audience with the power to change the content on the screen.

Or in a more recent example, the opportunity for the audience to binge-watch TV series can be a feature for a streaming service, but the unintended consequences are unfavorable for the business. You are producing expensive content to be consumed like fast food[132]. Let me explain it.

In traditional TV, seasons with 22 or so episodes were released to cover not just 22 weeks of weekly releases but the remaining 30 weeks of the year of repetitions. In that way, your content was used and reused. Almost evergreen content like *Friends,* the successful TV comedy, is the ideal example of passive revenue for TV content.

With 22 episodes available for immediate consumption in streaming, the audience consumes the entire season in less than a month, wants more, and it doesn't play the episodes again. Bad business. No wonder Apple TV+, HBO, or Disney+

[131] Carey, John. *When Media Are New: Understanding the Dynamics of New Media Adoption and Use.* University of Michigan Press, 2010. https://doi.org/10.39 98/nmw.8859947.0001.001.

[132] Corona, Adolfo Ramírez. "6 Things Netflix Needs (Besides Turning off Autoplay)." *Medium* (blog), March 5, 2020. https://adolforismos.medium .com/thanks-for-stopping-autoplay-but-whats-playing-next-netflix- a292131a11d8.

are releasing their new TV series one episode per week[133].

Risk management

Innovation is disruptive by nature, and sometimes innovators try to be more disruptive than normal to generate opportunities.

In the case of the side effects of TV series or googling you just have to pay attention to your product, make corrections, and take advantage of opportunities.

The problem is when unexpected and unintentional side effects emerge once the product or service is in the market and they are adverse to users, consumers, or audiences, like in the case of fast news, social networks, or digital addiction.

Pharmaceutical companies are a good example of how to manage risk in the development of new drugs. The care they put into the manufacture of their products before distribution is very well known — a lot of trials, reviewed processes, research...

But there are two particular things other industries can learn from them.

First, recognize that risk can be reduced but not disappear because there are things you can only know until the product is in the market.

Second, to mitigate the risk you have to consider the post-marketing process and invest as much in the collection, detection, assessment, monitoring, and prevention of adverse effects once the product is in the market as you did before its

---

[133] Alexander, Julia. "Disney Is Leading the Charge against Netflix by Returning to Weekly Episode Releases." The Verge, August 29, 2019. https://www.the verge.com/2019/8/29/20831410/disney-plus-apple-hulu-netflix-binge-episodes-full-season-drop-vs-weekly-release-streaming-model.

public consumption.

That is called pharmacovigilance[134] and other industries designing and developing products and services have a lot to learn from it.

But that's the subject of another story.

(Published on Aug 3, 2020, in UX Collective)

---

[134] "Pharmacovigilance." In *Wikipedia*, April 12, 2023. https://en.wikipedia.or g/w/index.php?title=Pharmacovigilance&oldid=1149424225.

27

You must start seeing content as a product: see these 3 cases

Don't treat it like a second-class citizen in design and production

Seeing content as a product can help you to improve your processes and the value of your products.

Usually, we see content just as a product companion, support, or asset to add to the final product. In other words, content is part of the marketing, instruction manuals, or another design element.

Except for books, music, movies, video games, or comics, that are not based on content or use the content as an asset: content is the product.

But any content can be viewed as a product. Particularly, any digital content can be viewed as a digital product.

If you see it from this perspective, content can be ideated, designed, generated, produced, distributed, and sold, as any product.

So, instead of sending a requirement of content to a copy-writer, you can see the required content as a product itself under any product management approach.

For example, your content can be part of an Agile methodology: write, publish, test, iterate, repeat.

> *Agile is an iterative approach to project management and software development that helps teams deliver value to their customers faster and with fewer headaches. Instead of betting everything on a "big bang" launch, an agile team delivers work in small, but consumable, increments. Requirements, plans, and results are evaluated continuously so teams have a natural mechanism for responding to change quickly. —via What is Agile? at Atlassian site*[135]

You can do that with other forms of content, like serialized fiction. The book "Write. Publish. Repeat." by Sean M. Platt and Johnny Truant was one of the first to describe independent publication of fiction novels as if you were developing and launching software.

The Agile frameworks can't be applied to any kind of content production, of course. For example, long novels, movies, and video games are designed and produced to get a final product, not as a minimum viable product or MVP with testing and iteration.

Anyway, the advantage to see the creation of content as a product is in process and value. You can produce better content

---

[135] Atlassian. "What Is Agile?" Atlassian. Accessed May 25, 2023. https://www.atlassian.com/agile.

that adds to a better product. Let's see this in the cases where we usually use content in products.

1. Content as a product companion

Moleskin (first a notebook manufacturer, now a product design company) is a brand that works very well with this kind of content. They started producing a physical product, a notebook, that was accompanied by a mythical story of its origin. Even today, every notebook comes with a little booklet narrating the story of other writers using them throughout history.

2. Content as product support

Instruction manuals and documentation fall into this category. For developers, for example, one important aspect to consider before adopting new technology is how well-documented it is.

But you can see the importance of content as product support in instruction manuals by Ikea, the furniture company. They have become a paradigm in instruction manuals designs. And end-users love them.

3. Content as an asset

This has become very relevant now with the rise of app development. All the text in UI is part of this category. We use to know it as UX writing even when all writing is UX writing. This content is seen as another element or ingredient to add to the elaboration of a product.

Of the three, this last one is the most integrated into the design process in some industries like software and tech. Ergo, it's, in some way, content already seen as a product.

Remember

We have to avoid handling content as a second citizen in our product design and production. Any content that you see as a product can be better and more effective, no matter if its apparent function is only to explain how to assemble a table.

(Published on Jul 19, 2021, in Concepts Against Reality)

28

The role of the designer in the era of smart speakers

Are you ready to design with your eyes closed?

What is going to be the function of the designer when the voice assistants and its audio apps domain the market?

Smart speakers are not the future. They are the present. The adoption has started[136]. It's just a matter of time, they are going to be ubiquitous.

Today most of the apps we can find on the different platforms (Amazon Echo, Apple HomePod, Google Home) are extensions of apps originally developed and launched for the smartphone and tablet market.

But this is going to end very soon. Apps originally developed

---

[136] Voicebot.ai. "Smart Speaker Sales to Rise 35% Globally in 2019 to 92 Million Units, 15 Million in China, Growth Slows," September 24, 2019. https://voicebot.ai/2019/09/24/smart-speaker-sales-to-rise-35-globally-in-2019-to-92-million-units-15-million-in-china-growth-slows/.

for smart speakers are going to be the norm.

The product managers and designers are thinking to adapt their products, but soon they are going to think about new audio and voice-based products.

The transition is interesting because we usually think of a product as a physical product. Even when it is an app, we start with prototypes, wireframes, or mockups to set a user flow.

Until today, the design has been very visual. There are exceptions, of course, but if we check stories or articles about user experience or design, written by UX and design experts, almost all of them talk about visual elements or involve in some way our vision.

Design is a big word, of course. Design is more than visual or graphic design. Product design, for example, is very complex for some products. And with the emergence of the user experience specialization, the field of the designer has become wider.

But let's face it, the audio part of any digital product or app was usually left to musicians, DJs, sound engineers, and just in recent years, to sound designers. It was left apart.

Let's remember the famous story of the origin of the Windows 95 startup sound. Those six seconds of music were composed by the producer and musician Brian Eno. The Microsoft people hired him with a very specific but hilarious briefing.

> *The thing from the agency said, 'We want a piece of music that is inspiring, universal, blah-blah, da-da-da, optimistic, futuristic, sentimental, emotional,' this whole list of adjectives, and then at the bottom it said 'and it must be 3.25 seconds long.' I thought this was so*

*funny and an amazing thought to actually try to make a
little piece of music—Brian Eno*[137]

Now, the sounds or music in the design of the user experience
can't be an extra element commissioned out of the design team
or process, like the Windows 95 startup sound.

Original Windows 95 wallpaper

Perhaps the industry with more knowledge and experience
in this area is the industry of video games where the sound
and music are as important or more than the rest of the visual
design. And even the game designers are going to need to think
about games completely sound-based.

I see three important areas where the designer is going to be
involved in the era of smart speakers.

---

[137] The Music Network. "The Odd Story of How Brian Eno Composed the
Windows 95 Startup Sound," July 30, 2021. https://themusicnetwork.com/
the-odd-story-of-how-brian-eno-composed-the-windows-95-startu
p-sound/.

Apps live everywhere

Even when we are going to find apps developed originally for the smart speakers' ecosystem, there is always some space for interaction with some kind of visual interface or control.

Some of the Amazon Echo skills (the name for apps in that ecosystem) can be configured with detail in the smartphone or tablet app for that skill.

The design has to take care of the coherence between the voice, the audio interactions, and the visual interface. "Do we have to use high-contrast colors with a soft female voice?" "Does the app look casual and spontaneous but the voice speaks formal and serious?"

And the apps can live everywhere besides the smartphone and the smart speaker: smartwatches, smart cars, tracking gadgets... Any of these devices may need a visual interface.

The designer as a whole user experience designer

The design of the user experience is going to be tested to its limits with the smart speakers' adoption.

The wireframes, prototypes, and visual user flows, are going to be in the past. We have to start thinking about new tools to design the user experience. Or rethink the tools we already have.

In the beginning, there were no considerations for the family experience on Netflix or Spotify. Today the same happens for Amazon Echo.

When you have a newborn in your family, you use your Spotify account to play a lot, I mean, a lot of baby's and children's music. And a baby can't have her own profile on Spotify so it is

198

really frustrating to receive music recommendations based on what you play and not what I really listen to.

Now with Amazon's Alexa in our home, every family member asks for a different kind of music. There is a way to change profiles or even music accounts but you don't think to do it when you just want to play music. So, my Spotify profile now recommends music based on the taste of my wife, my teenage daughter, and my three-year-old daughter.

(Amazon is implementing a voice recognition system that may solve this problem. In this way, Alexa can change the profile in use just by listening to the voice commanding her. We'll see.)

Designing with your eyes closed

At some moment and on some level, the designer will need to close his eyes.

Like those group exercises when you have to walk around blindfolded—sometimes with the help of others—other times alone, just to experience the absence of our main sense and forcing us to appreciate the touch, hear, smell and taste senses, the design process will have to experience the same.

The voice and sound have form, color, size, and texture... and can be a part of a system that requires space, composition, rhythm, movement...

To perceive and design all these elements, the designer will have to leave the visual comfort where he has been.

As a user, I want to see... I mean, to hear the new generation of apps designed originally for smart speakers, totally voice and sound-based.

199

I want to be surprised like when I experienced the first apps that really started to use the particular advantages of the smartphone, like the accelerometers, light sensors, camera, microphone, touch screen...

And as a professional involved in the conception, design, and development of software, I'm ready to close my eyes. Are you?

(Published on Dec 6, 2019, in UX Collective)

29

The best app on your smartphone nobody is talking about

Need a cue? Call me

There is a phone app nobody talks about anymore.

It's so good, it's almost never updated.

It's the app with one of the best UX and UI designs of all time.

The user experience is great:

- **Very useful**: everybody requires this app.
- **Highly usable**: no manual needed, grandma and her grand-children can use it.
- **Super findable**: the UI has it all at the tip of your fingers.
- **Extremely credible**: when similar apps fail, you open it.
- **Somewhat desirable**: it's the reason you bought the smart-phone in the first place.
- **Remarkably accessible**: no one was left behind.
- **Deeply valuable**: you can never delete this app.

And the user interface is every designer's dream:

- **Clear**: it's so clear, you don't notice it.
- **Concise**: every element is where it should be, no extras, no fancy adornments.
- **Familiar**: the only app my dad knew how to use on his first smartphone.
- **Responsive**: no loading spinners, fast, you feel every interaction.
- **Consistent**: You can buy a new phone or change to another operative system, and still use it as if nothing has happened.
- **Efficient**: fulfills the function of an interface — connects you to the main device.

It's one of the most used apps on smartphones, but every time new smartphones are presented every year, no one says a word.

Yet, the iPhone product page[138] doesn't mention anything about it.

Meet the Phone app

You may guess at this point: the best app on your smartphone is the phone app. No, not the phone, **the phone app**. Two different things.

It may sound ridiculous, but we have forgotten that the main function of a smartphone is the telephone function.

---

[138] Apple. "IPhone." Accessed May 25, 2023. https://www.apple.com/iphone/
.

The phone app works only as an interface to access the telephone, the duplex device that connects to a dedicated network transforms voice into electric signals, and the electric signals sound again, within a bidirectional and simultaneous transmission to the other end.

The interface is very old and it has become universal and standard. Most of its elements have been established in physical telephones since the 1930s[139].

But in terms of the user experience, the phone app is like good music in a film: it's not the protagonist; it's the support for a higher and final goal.

Image from Apple

Interface ≠ Experience

You use the phone app to make and receive telephone calls. That's it. Like the first rule of the *Fight Club*, you don't talk about it.

The main experience for the user is the use of the telephone.

---

[139] "Telephone." In *Wikipedia*, May 11, 2023. https://en.wikipedia.org/w/index.php?title=Telephone&oldid=1154267814.

Nothing is going to give the user the opportunity to contact a loved one, a family member, or a friend... with the richness of the human voice and the reliance on proven technology.

There have been improvements and alternatives. Most messaging apps like Whatsapp now have phone calls over the internet. You can switch from a phone call to a video call in the same phone app. Or the phone app may offer to record your calls very soon[140].

But when all the messaging apps or similar fail, you still open the phone app.

Aesthetically, the app left the skeuomorphism and got into the flat design. But essentially, the phone app remains the same.

iPhone 2007 Keynote

In an era where we see interfaces everywhere, it is interesting to have an app that does what it needs to do while its UI remains in oblivion.

The interface is not always the main protagonist in the user

---

[140] Michail. "Google Phone App Could Soon Offer Call Recording Option." GSMArena.com. Accessed May 25, 2023. https://www.gsmarena.com/google_phone_app_could_soon_offer_call_recording_option-news-41041.php.

experience. When you design the door [141]for a family home, nobody is going to stop to look at your door design, no matter how beautiful: family—the best experience—is inside, waiting for the user to go through.

Nobody wants to get in the way.

(Published on Feb 1, 2020, in UX Collective)

---

[141] Morgan, Jesse Russell. "Intro to UX: The Norman Door." Medium, January 23, 2019. https://uxdesign.cc/intro-to-ux-the-norman-door-61f8120b6 086.

30

The future of the smartphone is not the smartphone

Better camera? Better virtual assistant? Foldable screen?
Multitask screen? What is the future of the smartphone? We are
looking in the wrong direction

We are waiting for the spectacular announcement of the new smartphone just to repeat the experience of 2007 when the historical presentation of the new iPhone[142] made its appearance: the thrilling feeling that you are watching something that is going to change everything.

So, is it going to be the camera, the assistant, the foldable

---

[142] "IPhone (1st Generation)." In *Wikipedia*, May 22, 2023. https://en.wikipedi
a.org/w/index.php?title=IPhone_(1st_generation)&oldid=1156446493.

screen, the services, the apps, the payments[143]...

But, look around. Look at the forest, not the tree. Look at society. Look at human beings. This cannot be right.

(Adapted from Image by mohamed Hassan[144] and by Tkgd2007[145])

We are looking in the wrong direction. Literally.

I think the future of the smartphone is not the smartphone. Let me explain myself.

---

[143] Fowler, Geoffrey A. "Review | Whoa! Meet the Future Phones That Fold up, Have 9 Cameras and Charge over Thin Air." *Washington Post*, December 23, 2019. https://www.washingtonpost.com/technology/2018/06/29/whoa-meet-future-phones-that-fold-up-have-cameras-charge-over-thin-air/.

[145] "Download Free Media from Mohamed_hassan | Pixabay." Accessed May 25, 2023. https://pixabay.com/users/mohamed_hassan-5229782/.

[145] Tkgd2007. *English: A Silhouette of Human Evolution Created in Adobe Illustrator.* July 14, 2008. Own work. https://commons.wikimedia.org/w/index.php?curid=4375648.

A little bit of history

This may be a little controversial: the contemporary smart-phone is a circumstantial invention and adoption in our present culture.

If we review the history of the smartphone we can find an inflection point in the exit of the first iPhone to the market. Well, that was circumstantial.

What we knew before that moment is that in some way the computers were going to be smaller and smaller. That the internet was going to be available almost anywhere through those smaller computers.

Before the iPhone, we didn't know if the production of adoption of this premise was going to be in a new gadget or integrated with an old one.

I mean, where was the personal computer going to be? In a new little box? On a watch? On a little laptop? On glasses?

For user adoption, a new invention uses objects or gadgets already adopted. The motorized cars[146] were (and are) children of the horse-powered cars in size, design, use, etc. It would have been difficult to insert a different kind of motorized vehicle into a culture that has already adopted the wagons.

The personal computer was (and is) the child of the TV screen and the typewriter in terms of usability. Even if you could have invented some kind of iPad or tablet instead of the personal computer it would have been difficult to insert it into common daily use.

---

[146] "History of the Automobile." In *Wikipedia*, May 16, 2023. https://en.wikipedia.org/w/index.php?title=History_of_the_automobile&oldid=1155052300.

It may not have been a cell phone

When I was a child (forty years ago) there was a trend in digital and electronic watches. The combination between the LCD screen and the miniaturization of the chips and microcontrollers brought a new kind of watch.

The most basic was a little calculator, but then the calculator with little games came to the market, watches with different time zones, currency converters, note-taking functions, infinite calendars, voice recorders, etc.

In that moment of history, it looked like the watch was going to be the object through which technology and communication were going to be adopted in our daily life.

Yes, there is now the smartwatch and time seems to rematch this object, but...

...first was the iPhone

The most important thing to recall about the iPhone invention is that it was, first of all, a phone. Yes. We forget that sometimes.

It wasn't intended to have what we now call *apps*.

"The full Safari engine is inside of iPhone. And so, you can write amazing Web 2.0 and Ajax apps that look exactly and behave exactly like apps on the iPhone. And these apps can integrate perfectly with iPhone services. They can make a call, they can send an email, they can look up a location on Google Maps.

> *And guess what? There's no SDK that you need! You've*
> *got everything you need if you know how to write apps*

using the most modern web standards to write amazing apps for the iPhone today. So developers, we think we've got a very sweet story for you. You can begin building your iPhone apps today."—Steve Jobs, Mac World 2007[147]

(And yes again, we now have web progressive apps that are rematching Steve Jobs' vision, but we didn't know that in the beginning.)

The first iPhone was a child of the iPod and the cell phone. You bought an iPhone because you needed a cell phone or to replace the one you were using.

Even when you had a marvelous operative system and a microprocessor, it was a cell phone. So, in some way, the first iPhone was an enhanced phone. Nobody could anticipate the future of the smartphone in 2007.

In some sense, the first iPhone was an MVP (minimum viable product) that has been changing during all this time.

In the recent presentation on the latest iPhone 11, there wasn't any mention of the phone function of the gadget. Some people even think that we may have to stop calling it a phone. It's a camera, it's a computer, it's an assistant. And just sometimes we use it as a phone.

---

[147] *Safari: IPhone Development Platform*, 2007. https://www.youtube.com/watch?v=8Vq993Td6ys.

Reinventing from zero the... whatever a smartphone is

A very good exercise could be to reinvent the smartphone from zero but the truth is that we can take the *phone* part out of the equation.

In the list of what a smartphone is or what we use it for, the phone is maybe one of the last of the uses. I mean the cellular phone that uses a protocol that was intended to be compatible with the traditional phone (the one that used to use cable, remember?) because now we have VoIP (voice over internet protocol).

The smartphone needs an internet connection that is over the cellular phone connection (which is called cellular data protocol). But today, in terms of usability, what is the difference between using VoIP in any app on any computer, laptop or tablet and using an actual phone to talk to somebody?

For example, the new version of Whatsapp uses VoIP when you try to call someone inside the app and many people don't notice it. Or Alexa can be used as a phone in the home.

So, if we start to invent a smartphone today these are the requirements or the briefing:

- Some kind of personal computer.
- With an operative system so you can connect, extend or install interfaces of apps.
- With input senses: camera, microphone, sensors, GPS, etc.
- With high communication access to the Internet and all its protocols for data and voice.
- With access to the content of the Internet through a standard browser.

211

· With a virtual personal assistant.

In a sentence, we want a very personal, even intimate object that is intelligent and is the communication access point to almost any information or content, small, portable, and almost invisible in terms of use.

The only problem here in deciding which way we can go to start the design is to answer one question: what main interface are we gonna use?

Today, the main interface is a touchable screen. It was a very good option in the beginning but, is it an option now? Ask your neck.

Doing this exercise to reinvent the smartphone from zero we can see more clearly why the tendencies in the market:

· Audio interface: yes, that's the reason for Alexa, Google Home, and Apple Home, but also the Airpods.
· Screen as a second layer of our eyesight: here come the smart glasses.
· Watch: the return of the watch is here with the Apple Watch as the best example. But it may be some kind of bracelet.
· Multiple objects: smart assistants in the car, home, kitchen, phone, etc., under one name and service. With the IoT (Internet of Things) you have the requirements distributed in more than one object.

We can still use the touchable screen, of course. But not all the time.

So, as you see, that's why I think that the future of the smartphone is not the smartphone. I think that the smartphone we are using today is going to be useless or obsolete in ten years.

Well, maybe not for everyone, but most of us. Like any process of new technology adoption.

To find the next smartphone you have to stop looking down and look up. The next smartphone may have a different form than a smartphone, it may be in places or objects that you are already using, and you may interact with it in different ways than now: listening, talking, augmenting your reality, who knows...

(Published on Oct 28, 2019,in UX Collective)

About the Author

Adolfo Ramírez Corona is a vibrant writer, thinker, and multi-talented individual who seamlessly combines his passions for philosophy, technology, and the arts. With a diverse background spanning teaching, photography, and consultancy, Adolfo's unique perspectives captivate readers and inspire profound introspection. Born in Mexico City, his explorations in philosophy and aesthetics fuel his insightful writings, while his work as a photojournalist and consultant sharpens his keen eye for detail and understanding of the human experience.

In addition to his vibrant career, Adolfo Ramírez Corona embraces a variety of artistic pursuits, finding solace in literature, photography, and visual arts. His insatiable thirst for knowledge extends to extensive reading, ranging from philosophical works to cutting-edge texts on technology and business. Through profound inspiration wielded by literary and philosophical giants like Calvino, Borges, Nietzsche, and Gladwell, Adolfo Ramírez Corona's words paint vivid portraits of our complex world, leaving readers both captivated and enlightened.

Presently, Adolfo Ramírez Corona leads the charge as the visionary mind behind a groundbreaking streaming TV channel, seamlessly blending his expertise with his love for the ever-evolving landscape of media and technology. Join him on a transformative journey through his works, where the power of thought converges with the beauty of the present, offering readers an opportunity to delve into the depths of their own minds and discover profound truths about the human experience.

You can connect with me on:
- 🌐 https://adolforismos.com
- 🐦 https://twitter.com/adolforismos
- 🔗 https://adolforismos.medium.com

Subscribe to my newsletter:
- ✉ https://adolforismos.substack.com

Also by Adolfo Ramírez Corona

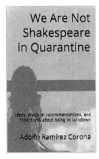

We Are not Shakespeare in Quarantine

This is not King Lear or Macbeth. You will not find the development of a new calculus.

Instead, you will go through ideas and stories about our emotions, lessons from a little prince, challenging decisions, anxiety, remote work, working with children at home, videoconferences, challenges in the new normal, the post-pandemic crisis, the future, post-traumatic growth, and how to escape lockdown.

We are not Shakespeare in quarantine. But we are not alone either.

Made in the USA
Coppell, TX
01 November 2023

23695070R00127